THE ARGUMENT TOOLBOX

K.J. PETERS

broadview press

BROADVIEW PRESS – www.broadviewpress.com
Peterborough, Ontario, Canada

Founded in 1985, Broadview Press remains a wholly independent publishing house. Broadview's focus is on academic publishing; our titles are accessible to university and college students as well as scholars and general readers. With over 800 titles in print, Broadview has become a leading international publisher in the humanities, with world-wide distribution. Broadview is committed to environmentally responsible publishing and fair business practices.

Library and Archives Canada Cataloguing in Publication

Title: The argument toolbox / K.J. Peters.
Names: Peters, K. J. (Kevin J.), author.
Description: Includes bibliographical references and index.
Identifiers: Canadiana (print) 20210378395 | Canadiana (ebook) 20210378425 | ISBN 9781554815166
    (softcover) | ISBN 9781770488465 (PDF) | ISBN 9781460407936 (EPUB)
Subjects: LCSH: English language—Rhetoric.
Classification: LCC PE1408 .P4674 2022 | DDC 808/.042—dc23

Broadview Press handles its own distribution in North America:
PO Box 1243, Peterborough, Ontario K9J 7H5, Canada
555 Riverwalk Parkway, Tonawanda, NY 14150, USA
Tel: (705) 743-8990; Fax: (705) 743-8353
email: customerservice@broadviewpress.com

For all territories outside of North America, distribution is handled by Eurospan Group.

Broadview Press acknowledges the financial support of the Government of Canada for our publishing activities.

Canada

Edited by Martin R. Boyne

Book design by Chris Rowat Design

PRINTED IN CANADA

THE
ARGUMENT
TOOLBOX

CONTENTS

PREFACE

Drawing upon the pedagogy, rhetorical theory, and student editor insights of *The Argument Handbook*, *The Argument Toolbox* is designed to help first-year composition students, rhetoric and writing students, and first-year seminar students build persuasive arguments in various genres and blended genres.

STUDENT EDITORS

It has been a long time since I was a student, so I didn't have a student's perspective and didn't understand their experiences until I asked. The students below shared their time and helped me understand what I didn't know. These students, drawn from colleges and universities across North America, became the Board of Student Editors. Their insights were indispensable to the development of the examples and features and the selection of models throughout.

Alexa Faye Rhein Aaronson	Mekleit Dix
Alma Acosta	Elicia Flemming
Wenmar Pagulayan Badbada	Peyton Gajan
Sabrina Barreto	Sneha Gandhi
Nina Batt	Daneil Gherardi
Jamie Battaglia	Hannah Gioia
Dominick Beaudine	Laurne Glass
Christopher Caruso	Elizabeth Goldhammer
Eric Chavoya	Alvaro Gonzalez
Christopher Chien	Kelly Hu
Cole D. Crawford	Katherine Kennedy
Caroline de Bie	Christine Kilicarslan
Hilda Delgadillo	Oscar King IV

Alec Lee	Kathleen Porter
Olivia Li	Lauren Roknich
Nicole Lindars	Nikolas Romero
Audrey Liviakis	Anthony Sasso
Sonja Lorance	Alyssa Smith
Hudson Luthringshausen	Cedar Smith
Zachary Malinski	Jacqueline Smith
Tyler Marting	Riley Stauffer
Hannah Maryanski	John Tavelli
Kaya McMullen	Jenna Thomas
Laura Miola	Raven Tukes
Yulissa Nunez	Brendan Viloria
Veronica Pacheco	Adonis Williams
Alexandra Petosa	Nick A. Yim
Alexia Pineda	Vanessa Zavala-Zimmerer

What did they teach me? Well, they helped me realize that those who intentionally plagiarize probably aren't reading assigned chapters. However, good students are worried about mistakes that may lead to an accusation of plagiarism. The student board members also helped me understand their questions and challenges, such as the pressure of managing not one but multiple research writing assignments in very different courses given by diverse professors with very tight deadlines.

Surprisingly, some of my own experiences as a student were mirrored in the student editors. For example, whenever a new idea was introduced to me in class, my first question was, why do I need to know this? Similarly, many board members expressed disappointment with professors who cannot justify what they are teaching and with texts that do not bother to describe the value of what they present. For this reason, each chapter begins with a justification of the subject and a brief discussion of its purpose and value.

More to the point, the Board of Student Editors helped me understand that at 1:20 a.m. when working on a paper that just isn't coming together, they don't have time to read an entire chapter to remind themselves how to integrate a source. Instead, they need good information built on solid pedagogy, and relevant advice—and they need it all fast.

MODULAR ORGANIZATION

Like the more comprehensive text, *The Argument Toolbox* retains the handbook format so that students can zero in on the content they need to respond to an assignment when faced with a blank screen, a hard deadline, and a skeptical audience. And professors can select and assign content that fits their course plan.

APPROACH: THREE LENSES FOR VIEWING ARGUMENTS

The Editorial Board helped me see that students attending very different colleges and universities often struggled with similar issues and concepts. For example, students enjoy **invention** exercises, but many don't think it is worth the time when time is tight. **Audience** is a consideration that many students don't give a second thought, partly because high schools have always provided a specific, well-defined audience: the teacher. However, colleges and universities provide students an array of professorial expectations shaped by disciplines, specialties, and individual dispositions. Finally, when one member of the board said, "how can I speak with **authority** if I don't have a degree yet?" I was surprised to discover that many students believe an authoritative voice and presence are beyond their grasp.

To help students understand and integrate these concepts into their writing process, *The Argument Toolbox* is based on three lenses for viewing argument and focuses on examples relevant to today's students:

- **Invention**: From the very beginning, the book expands the sources of invention beyond an individual's memory and experiences to include peers, genres, and the conventions of specific disciplines, as well as libraries and archives. Students learn to see how ideas are informed by evidence, how evidence is understood, and why research is necessary.
- **Audience**: Throughout, the book helps students see persuasion in real-world terms instead of a static classroom assignment. The lens of audience teaches students to look for audience expectations in an email or a lab-report assignment, for example, and it helps students see different genres as ways of meeting the varied expectations of very different audiences.
- **Authority**: To succeed in academic writing as well as in other writing situations, students need to understand genre and disciplinary practices such as sourcing and documentation as ways of building and expressing persuasive power. As they learn the importance of establishing authority in their writing, students will come to see building trust as essential.

TOOLBOXES

The insights of the student board of editors helped in the development of "Toolboxes": three types of brief, boxed commentaries intended to help students make sense of and apply concepts to their own writing.

- **Breaking the Block** boxes provide step-by-step activities to help students who are at a loss for something to say. Students are often stopped by mental, structural, organizational, tonal, and phrasing blocks that stop invention, drafting, and revision. Additionally, this set of boxes helps students see revision, research, and experimenting with genres and constrictions as forms of invention that can impel greater creativity and clarity of voice.

- **Conventions in Context** boxes focus on how audience expectations can dictate the use of conventions in any given situation. For example, in Module V-5, the box provides an understanding of how an environmental sciences professor and a theology professor use cause-and-effect arguments differently.
- **Responsible Sourcing** boxes help students see documentation and sourcing as means of building trust and authority. These boxes also include practical advice such as strategies writers use to keep track of their sources.

ACKNOWLEDGEMENTS

Looking back, I now understand the leap of faith Marjorie Mather and Broadview Press took in accepting my manuscript. I am grateful for their support and honored to be part of the Broadview catalog. And I am embarrassed that I did not express the debt I owe to Carla Samodulski, Christopher Bennem, and Lisa Moore. Ms. Samodulski, Mr. Bennem, and Ms. Moore gifted me their time and talents. Thanks to these friends and my editors at Broadview Press, when I read powerful, beautiful, and persuasive writing, I think of the editors that made it so.

Most of all, my love and thanks to Robin and Eliza. You are my motivation. If you are a student and have read this far, thank you and best of luck. And if you happen to have a student named Eliza Peters in your class, you would do well to listen to her as she is brilliant, has great advice, and you would be lucky to be her friend. If you find yourself in Dr. Miskolzce's class, count yourself lucky to be in the presence of a gifted scholar with a beautiful mind.

CHAPTER 1

BUILDING ARGUMENTS: AN INTRODUCTION

MODULE I-1

ARGUMENT DEFINED

An **argument** is an attempt to persuade someone to think, believe, or act differently by offering reasons in support of a conclusion. Successful arguments persuade readers or listeners to change an opinion, a belief, or a behavior. In this module, we will examine some of the broadest categories of and reasons for argument and discuss some strategies for writing arguments. We'll also take a look at the type of argument of most immediate concern to students: academic arguments.

Strategies for Argument

Whatever their purpose and subject, writers of compelling arguments employ strategies, or tricks of the trade, to persuade audiences. Some basic strategies include appeals to readers' or listeners' tendency to trust authority, appeals to their emotions, and the use of different types of reasoning.

Three ways to appeal to an argument's audience. Arguments are persuasive if they appeal to their intended audience, just as cooking a friend's favorite food for a birthday party is a way of appealing to her appetite and thereby communicating your feelings. The three common rhetorical appeals are described briefly below.

- **An ethical appeal, or** *ethos*, involves an author or speaker moving the audience to believe that the source of the message is trustworthy and authoritative. It is an effective strategy because an audience tends to trust writers and speakers who are authorities on the issue at hand. Citing recognized experts in a field, including the academic degrees and publishing record of a source, and carefully documenting your sources using a widely accepted documentation style, such as the system recommended by the Modern Language Association (MLA) or the American Psychological Association (APA), are ways of making an ethical appeal.
- **An emotional appeal, or** *pathos*, does just what it says: it appeals to the emotions of the audience in an attempt to move its members to think, believe, or act differently. For example, the SPCA shows images of animals in distress to provoke pity and thereby motivate the audience to send in a donation.
- **A logical appeal, or** *logos*, relies upon logical reasoning and verifiable evidence to persuade. Most logical appeals are based on two types of reasoning: inductive and deductive.

Types of Reasoning or Logic

Reasoning is a means of connecting the evidence you have discovered to your conclusion, using logic. The two types of reasoning described below are commonly used in a wide variety of arguments.

- **Inductive reasoning** starts with observations about the world or your surroundings; you then use these observations to draw a conclusion that you believe is probably true. Induction is an exploratory form of reasoning because it can lead to previously undiscovered conclusions.
- **Deductive reasoning** uses one or more rules or general truths to come to a conclusion. Unlike induction, deduction involves the application of known truths or undisputed knowledge.

Chapter 5 describes in detail many different types of arguments and ways to approach your subject and engage your audience. Chapter 5 also includes a number of useful strategies that can help you build persuasive arguments. Although you no doubt make many arguments in your daily life and at work, the type of argument you are probably most concerned about as you read this is an academic argument.

Characteristics of Academic Arguments

An **academic argument** is a specialized way of persuading an audience to think, believe, or act differently for the vital purpose of advancing knowledge. The goal of an academic argument is not simply to win or persuade. Scholars construct arguments to find, develop, test, and contribute knowledge to the ongoing exploration and discussion among others in a discipline or specialty.

Different disciplines and professors have various specific requirements for a successful academic argument. In general, however, if you are going to join the discussion in a field by making your ideas public in an academic context, you need to know that your audience will expect an argument composed of the elements listed below.

- **A thesis**: Academic arguments are built around a clearly stated thesis, or conclusion, which the reasons and evidence support. The thesis is the assertion to be proved. It typically appears at the beginning of an argument and is often restated and expanded toward the end. However, a thesis comes together at the end, it is the conclusion, of the research process. Chapter 5 discusses thesis development for different forms and genres of argument.
- **Evidence**: Academic arguments include data and other types of information that are used to support the reasons that in turn support the thesis. Evidence must be acceptable, valid, and authoritative in the eyes of the audience if the reasons are to have any persuasive power.
- **Reasoning**: In academic contexts, reasoning is used to connect an argument's reasons (or 'premises') to its conclusion to demonstrate that the conclusion is true. The standards of reasoning and appropriate conclusions may vary from one discipline to another, even when the subject matter is the same. A biologist may reason toward a conclusion about the constitution of the human body, while a dance professor may reason toward a conclusion about the ideal movements of that body. In both cases, the subject is the human body, but the reasoning of the biologist is not like the reasoning of the dance professor.
- **Knowledge of the larger debate**: As stated above, academics argue to contribute to the ongoing exploration and discussion within a particular discipline. To join the conversation, the authors of an academic argument must demonstrate that they know what has already been said (discovered or disputed) by other scholars. Also, they must show why their ideas are relevant and how they contribute to the larger debate.
- **Adherence to conventions**: **Conventions** is another term for the grammar, punctuation, style, format, and tone that adherents of an academic discipline or specialty will expect. Though all disciplines have some conventions in common, such as spelling, different disciplines have different expectations. An argument that does not correctly use the conventions scholars or professors expect will not be persuasive and may suggest that the author or speaker is not ready to join the conversation.

Non-Academic Arguments

Not all arguments are academic. Many discussions in popular media may not be seen as persuasive by an academic audience or welcome in an academic setting. For example, **debates**, in which two people or two teams try to "score points," declare their opinions, or play to the crowd, can be a setting for arguments. However, debates may not be perceived as exploring or contributing to knowledge. **Quarrels**—angry disagreements—happen when people become frustrated with their inability to persuade and either forget to use or give up using reasons and evidence to support their points (see Figure 1.1). One familiar type of quarrel is common to cable TV panel discussions, which are more about the fireworks of clashing personalities than an attempt to discover truth using reasons and evidence. Academics are as passionate as any other profession; however, cool restraint is the expected demeanor of a seeker of knowledge.

Figure 1.1
Sometimes a quarrel just isn't worth the effort.

    Tweets or sound bites, features of media discussions as well as political campaigns, are summaries of positions or short assertions lacking evidence. Tweets or sound bites are closer to bumper stickers than reasoned argument because they lack evidence and reasoning.

    Some assertions and disputes are not arguments at all. Self-indulgence and bullying have no place in argument. Self-indulgent speakers talk to hear their own voice and brag about their accomplishments. Though such behavior can seem like an argument, it is rarely persuasive. Bullying or threatening the audience in some way also is not persuasive in any setting, but especially not in an academic setting because the bully is neither using reasons and evidence nor contributing knowledge.

Visual and Multimedia Arguments

Most of the time, academics and others use language to make arguments, but they can also make them using imagery, sound, and technology, as Steve Jobs did when he introduced the first iPhone. You can find videos of Jobs's presentation, titled "Reinvent the Phone," on YouTube. His "keynote" is still a good example of a persuasive multimedia argument.

Visual arguments such as the one in Figure 1.2, which are most frequently encountered outside of the academic world, may look very different from written arguments. Visual, multimedia, and textual arguments, however, are built for the same purpose and all are composed of reasons and evidence.

Figure 1.2
Terry Richardson's Equinox ads are provocative and have proven successful in targeting a specific clientele that understands fitness as fashion.

A **visual argument** makes use of elements such as imagery and text, negative and positive space, layout and color, as well as info-graphics such as charts and graphs to persuade someone to think, believe, or act differently. For example, the advertisement shown in Figure 1.2 makes a cause-and-effect argument. The strength of the man is caused "BY EQUINOX." More prominently, the ad would have you believe that the beauty of the woman demonstrating the same strength as the man is also a product of Equinox gyms.

You do not have to be a graphic designer or an advertiser to develop visual arguments. Each time you update your Instagram story with photos or graphics, you are using images and text to persuade others of your personality, qualities, likes, and dislikes.

As multimedia capabilities and tools become as common and easy to use as a smartphone, the expectations for persuasive visual arguments will increase. If you can build a strong argument, you can build a strong visual argument. For more on visual arguments, see Chapter 6.

Invention, Audience, and Authority: Three Lenses for Viewing Argument

Whether you are constructing a written or visual argument, and whatever the argument's context, it is natural to feel overwhelmed by the many decisions you have to make as you move through the process of composing a persuasive text. However, if you look at your task through these three lenses, a great deal of the noise and confusion will melt away:

Invention: Information retrieval and synthesis. In other words, what you find out about an **issue**—a matter about which people disagree—and how you put this information together.

Audience: The people you are attempting to persuade. Understanding the audience's thoughts and expectations is the key to your persuasive power.

Authority: Traits and qualities that establish your credibility, leading an audience to pay attention to and be persuaded by your argument.

Invention, audience, and authority are the essential perspectives that shape *The Argument Toolbox*.

Like any good toolbox, the chapters that follow will give you practical tools, tricks of the trade, time-saving exercises, and simple solutions to the problems that pop up whenever you try to build an argument.

MODULE I-2

INVENTION AND RESEARCH: HOW WILL YOU FIND IDEAS AND EVIDENCE?

Invention is the process of retrieving and synthesizing information and ideas in order to generate new perspectives, ideas, and arguments. An effective invention process suits an individual's style of composing and helps that writer move from frustration to inspiration and break writer's block. The type of information you seek and where it can typically be found should determine your invention process. When you retrieve the information from within your head, the invention process is called *looking within*. Chapter 2 presents invention strategies that will help you look within, including freewriting and imposing artificial limits on your writing. When you seek information outside your own thoughts and beyond your own experience, you are *looking around* by consulting friends and peers or going into the field to observe. Chapter 2 will also help you look around to invent. *Looking to research* helps you look beyond your immediate experience and the experiences of others that you consult to seek the ideas of scholars and other experts, that is, the authorities in the field. Chapter 2 will also help you locate and gather the ideas of scholars and experts, and help you analyze and evaluate what you have gathered so you can draw informed conclusions.

How Invention Saves Time and Effort

Whatever your composing task, you usually have only a limited period of time to complete it. Within that time, you must gather ideas and information, organize your material and write a draft, and then revise and proofread your writing. When you use one or more invention strategies to develop some ideas to work with, organizing, drafting, revising, and proofreading become much less daunting tasks.

However, the more time you spend looking at a blank page or procrastinating out of fear that you have nothing to say, the less time you will have for the other stages of the composing process. See the Breaking the Block box entitled "Invention Never Stops" for an invention strategy that can help you in this situation.

Breaking the Block
Invention Never Stops

Everyone experiences writer's block. It is important to remember that writer's block is not necessarily caused by a lack of ideas. Often, writers get stuck because they have too many ideas to choose from and too many potential audiences to talk to.

To overcome writer's block, you can use invention throughout the composing process. In addition, you are surrounded by the most valuable invention tool ever discovered—friends and peers.

INSTRUCTIONS: For one week, record your ideas as Step One describes, and then share them with others. Remember to include the day and time of each recorded thought.

Step One: Record Your Ideas

- Keep some means of recording your ideas near you at all times. It could be a notebook, a scrap of paper, or your smartphone's notes or voice memo app.

- Do not judge or dismiss any idea that comes to mind until you have kept it for a week and thought about it numerous times.
- When you have a great idea or a great question, or when you see something amazing, record your thoughts before they evaporate.

Step Two: Share Your Ideas

- Bounce your ideas off friends and peers.
- Write down or record how others respond to your ideas. Also, don't forget to write down your own thoughts and responses.
- Remember that critical responses are just opportunities to re-see and reshape your thinking.

Step Three: Give Your Ideas the Respect They Deserve

- At the end of the week, review all your notes or listen to the recordings you made.
- Look for connections between your ideas and observations and the responses of friends and peers.
- Categorize and prioritize the ideas and responses using some or all of the following, or other categories that seem appropriate to the task:
  - Big ideas I must develop now
  - Ideas related to big ideas
  - Thoughts that need time to develop
  - Problems to be solved
  - Solutions looking for a problem

How Writers Use Research to Discover Ideas

You may think that research consists simply of finding an assigned number of sources to support a thesis. Finding sources that confirm a pre-existing thesis is not research, however. Instead, research is a process of discovery.

Research is another kind of invention. When you conduct research, you internalize information outside of your own experience so that you can challenge and develop your understanding. Research is necessary because new ideas are built upon existing ideas. When you learn about the ideas of others, observe the world around you, and engage in critical thinking and conversations with knowledgeable sources, you will develop a deeper, more informed perspective on your subject, you will have more to say, and your argument will be more persuasive. In short, you do research to discover what you do not know so that you may know more.

When a student reads a scholarly article or when reporters review court records, they are doing research. Research is not limited to print sources such as scholarly books and papers, however. When a sculptor studies the anatomy of a hand, she is doing research. When the famous scientist, anthropologist, and author Jane Goodall observes chimpanzees in their natural habitat, she is doing research. There is no single way to do research. There are, however, good and bad research methods.

Researching How People Think and Talk

Through research, you will also gain an understanding of the expectations of your audience as you discover how your intended audience or those who work in a specific discipline or field think and talk about your subject. Use your understanding of how your audience thinks and what they expect to shape your argument.

Individuals in the film industry, for example, think and talk about *aspect ratios* and *medium shots*, whereas those in the computer industry talk about *LANs* and *bit rates*. If you are writing a paper for a history professor, clues to your professor's expectations will be found in the arguments written by other historians, or in the way that professor formulates her ideas in class.

Knowing how members of your audience think, what they value, and how they will understand you is as important as knowing what you want to say. When the writers of an episode of *CSI* want realism, they ask real crime scene investigators what word they would use to describe a piece of evidence and what procedures they would follow in a given situation. The writers of *CSI* also need to know the words a detective would *never* use to describe evidence. The audience of *CSI* expects realistic dialogue, and the writers do their best to meet this expectation. The same is true of the academic world.

Research helps you determine what you want to say and how to say it. Chapter 3 explains how to read the situation that you and your audience will share and how to discover audience expectations so that you can shape what you want to say appropriately and persuasively.

Using Invention and Research to Shape Your Voice and Authority

Invention and research provide ideas and ways to talk about those ideas. Research can also help you determine the evidence that an audience trusts, respects, and will listen to. Imagine that you are working on a new app for mobile devices that helps students prioritize their daily activities, and you need to make a pitch for it to three entirely different audiences: your friends, potential investors, and a software engineer.

Investors like those in *The Shark Tank* reality TV show will want to hear about the likelihood of sales and returns on investment. Your friends, on the other hand, might be interested in how the app will help them plan their day. However, if you are trying to describe the app's functions to a software engineer or an app developer, you may need to use technical terms to describe how the app will gather calendar data and then migrate it to an SMS (a Short Message Service on different devices.).

Research and reading in this area will not only help you understand how app developers talk but also help you join their conversation as a respected voice. Of course, an engineer can understand your app as your friends do, but if you can use the language an engineer uses and the information she respects, you and your ideas will have much more persuasive power and be more appropriate for the intended audience.

MODULE I-3

WHAT YOU NEED TO KNOW ABOUT WRITING IN UNIVERSITIES AND COLLEGES

Each university and college classroom is a different situation. And, you may discover the expectations in a single course may change day to day. One way to understand a situation like a classroom is to look at it rhetorically. A **rhetorical situation** consists of all the elements that affect how an audience understands an argument. The audience, writer/speaker, and message form a triangle at the heart of the rhetorical situation as illustrated on the left of Figure 1.3. The rhetorical situation of a classroom or lab is a bit different from other rhetorical situations, as illustrated on the right of Figure 1.3.

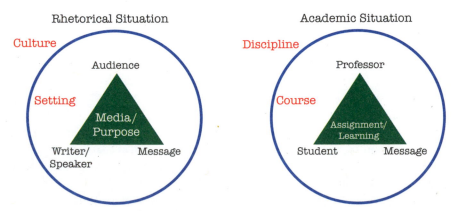

Figure 1.3 The complex rhetorical situations in an academic setting will reflect the discipline of your course and professor.

To break down the differences and similarities of a general rhetorical situation and an academic situation, see the side-by-side comparison in Figure 1.4.

All rhetorical situations exist within some larger cultural environment. As a student you work within the academic tradition; however, in a single course you need to focus on the cultural principles, values, and practices of the specific discipline that course represents.

There are many ways to define a **discipline**. As a student, the best way to think of a discipline is as the practices used by a group of scholars who

- are motivated to increase understanding and contribute to what is known;
- study a common subject or focus on a related set of questions;
- apply the same or similar habits of critical thinking, methods of discovery, and innovative practices; and
- communicate in and are organized by formal, specialized ways of exchanging and evaluating information.

General Rhetorical Situation / Academic Situation

Audience
The individual or group who will read, hear, or observe an argument.

Professor
The individual who teaches the course and evaluates you as a student.

Writer or Speaker
The one who creates and delivers the argument.

Student
You, the one studying a subject and doing assignments to be evaluated by the professor.

Purpose
The goal the writer or speaker hopes to achieve by persuading the audience to change opinions, principles, or behavior.

Learning
Demonstrating your understanding, skills, competencies, and knowledge in your work and contributions.

Setting
The time, place, and context where an audience encounters an argument.

Course
The specific academic setting where you study an aspect of a subject discipline and are then evaluated on your understanding by a professor.

Culture
Principles, values, and practices that make it possible for the individual to express ideas and experiences, and for an audience to understand these expressions.

Discipline
Similar or common methods of examining a subject, common habits of critical thinking, and formal ways of communicating that allow scholars to exchange and evaluate information and contribute to what is known.

Figure 1.4
Comparing a general rhetorical situation and an academic rhetorical situation reveals important differences.

You may have noticed that a physics professor and a creative writing professor do not teach in the same way. This is probably because they are different people, but mostly because they have years of study, training, and practice in different disciplines that lead them to think, do research, and teach differently.

No text can predict your professor's assignments or expectations. Therefore, relying on any sample paper, template, or outline (except those provided by your professor) is the same as ignoring your audience. For this reason, students who plagiarize papers are likely to be disappointed by their grade, even if their fraud is not discovered, because the author of a purchased paper has no idea what your professor expects in a specific course or assignment.

To understand your audience within the academic situation, you need to study your professor, learn her expectations, and understand the markers of authority in their discipline. The checklist in Figure 1.5 will help you examine the rhetorical situation of any class.

> ### . Investigate the rhetorical situation of your class
>
> 1. Study the discipline. Study the course description, syllabus, and textbook introduction because these are the clearest statements of the professor's vision for the course.
>
> 2. Read articles written by professors in the same subject area.
>
> 3. Investigate your professor. Read anything he or she has written, performed, or demonstrated that may reveal principles, methods, and practices the professor values, including articles, reviews, and blogs.
>
> 4. Interview your professor. Be direct. Ask about the course objectives as well as insights he or she hopes the class will learn.
>
> 5. Ask the professor for examples of assignments, templates of required writing, and any preferences for work turned in.
>
> 6. Ask classmates what they think the professor expects.
>
> 7. Ask students who have recently taken the same class what the professor expects and values in student work and writing.

Figure 1.5 Though each discipline is different, the expectations of professors and markers of authority are not secret, and they are easily investigated and understood.

Your audience, your professor, will read your sentences and paragraphs carefully. So too, will they read your use of the markers that communicate authority in an academic situation. **Authority** consists of the traits and qualities that lead an audience to pay attention to and be persuaded by an argument, thereby shaping the meaning within the situation. The Responsible Sourcing box entitled "Prioritizing Audience Saves Time and Grades" provides a way to think about your voice and authority.

Responsible Sourcing
Prioritizing Audience Saves Time and Grades

All students have to prioritize to save time and energy. Often, it's worth taking time to discover what your academic audience is looking for before spending time on an assignment.

Imagine it is late at night. You have homework in all your classes, a midterm essay to write, and little time. As you think about your next steps, you realize you have many options for the essay, but the results of those options may not be so clear. As the decision tree in Figure 1.6 shows, some decisions can take you where you want to go, while others can lead to less happy results.

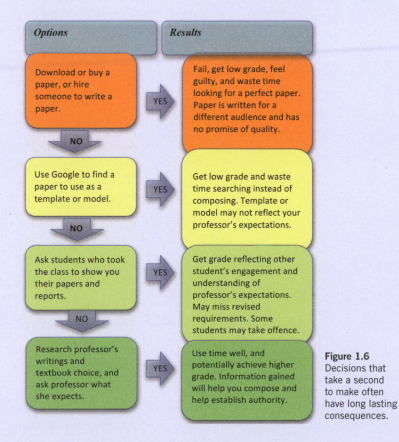

Options

Download or buy a paper, or hire someone to write a paper. — **YES** → Fail, get low grade, feel guilty, and waste time looking for a perfect paper. Paper is written for a different audience and has no promise of quality.

NO ↓

Use Google to find a paper to use as a template or model. — **YES** → Get low grade and waste time searching instead of composing. Template or model may not reflect your professor's expectations.

NO ↓

Ask students who took the class to show you their papers and reports. — **YES** → Get grade reflecting other student's engagement and understanding of professor's expectations. May miss revised requirements. Some students may take offence.

NO ↓

Research professor's writings and textbook choice, and ask professor what she expects. — **YES** → Use time well, and potentially achieve higher grade. Information gained will help you compose and help establish authority.

Results

Figure 1.6
Decisions that take a second to make often have long lasting consequences.

CHAPTER 2

INVENTING AND RESEARCHING ARGUMENTS

MODULE II-1

ELEMENTS OF EFFECTIVE INVENTION

Classical rhetoric provides one definition of **invention**—the discovery of the available means of persuasion. This definition and traditional methods of invention were designed to help individuals, working alone, draw upon their own experiences and memories. However, now we see that invention is a social act—new ideas come from groups brainstorming together or individuals engaging and playing with social norms, expectations, and traditions. For example, the musical mashups produced by contemporary DJs are extremely innovative. However, the source of their innovative sound is as much their own minds as it is the variety of songs they sample and arrange for a remix. If it were not for their brainstorming as they create beats, assemble samples, or play with different genres of music, DJs' distinctive sound would not exist.

Using Invention throughout the Writing Process

Invention isn't just the first stage of your writing process. As you develop an argument, invention provides the tools you need as you move from finding an issue to write about, to developing your ideas about the issue, to deciding on your position or the structure of your argument. As you can see in Figure 2.1, the following elements of an invention process can help writers solve problems and develop their arguments:

Problems . . .

You cannot get started with your writing assignment. You have a lot of 'ok' ideas, but none of them stand out.	Your idea is fuzzy, and you are not sure how to clarify your thoughts and make them relevant.	You have an issue to write about, but you have not yet decided on a position; you have a lot to say, but you need a way to organize your ideas.

Solutions . . .

BRAINSTORMING	QUESTIONS	GENRES & FORMS

Examples . . .

After 15 minutes of freewriting, you notice the word 'environment' keeps popping up.	Thinking of questions such as "How is car defined?" helps you move from abstract to concrete.	Using the genre of historical analysis, you write about the history of cars, which helps you decide on a position: automotive technology has changed as the environment has changed.
As a writing exercise, you try to write about the environment without using the word environment. You find that cars keep coming to mind.	Thinking in terms of cause and effect leads you to wonder, "Why do we only think of cars damaging the environment?"	Rewriting as an editorial, you link the history of engine technology to the history of air pollution, and then propose cars that clean the air as they are driven.

Figure 2.1 Using invention to develop an argument.

- **Brainstorming** is an umbrella term for a number of strategies that help you look within and around to access memories, to see how others perceive shared experiences, and to use group discussions to develop ideas. Like a data-mining software program, brainstorming strategies help you rediscover what you already know and combine ideas and memories to form new insights and opinions. In Module II-2, you will find seven brainstorming strategies.
- **Questions** can help you clarify your opinions by revealing your assumptions and attitudes. Asking questions about what at first appears to be a simple thought often yields great insight. In addition, if you are confused or unsure about an assignment, asking your professor can shed light on unstated expectations. More important, simply by asking questions you can turn writer's block into a problem-solving activity. Chapter 4 shows you how to use questions to clarify your argument.
- **Genres** are time-tested ways of structuring arguments. Examples of argument genres include editorials, proposals, and position papers. If you have a jumble of ideas and research notes, trying out various genres can give you different ways of seeing and defining the scope of your subject. For example, you can

frame the position that "manned exploration of Mars is practical" as a definition, an analysis, and an editorial to see which genre best suits your purpose for writing and your audience. See Chapter 5 for genres and forms that can help shape your argument.

Getting Comfortable with the Mess

Invention is the messy act of gathering the raw material of ideas so you can start thinking on the page—building and connecting ideas without judgment. If you are worried about neatness or grammatical correctness while using invention strategies, you will limit your creativity.

In fact a mess, like a counter full of ingredients, can lead to new combinations and new perspectives simply because in a mess very different items and ideas will be near each other. Just as a kitchen with a chaotic array of spices, unusual ingredients, and splatters of sauces on the wall and floor is a part of creating a new taste, a mess of ideas is a necessary condition of an effective invention strategy.

No Criticizing during Invention

A new idea is delicate. It can be killed by a sneer or a yawn; it can be stabbed to death by a quip and worried to death by a frown on the right man's [woman's] brow—Ovid

Do not judge an idea before its time. If you have ever spent an hour staring at a blank screen, or writing down a sentence only to erase it, you know the silencing power of self-criticism.

Because new ideas are delicate, they need time to grow. There will be time to criticize and judge later. As you practice the invention strategies in this chapter, remember that the goal is to let the ideas flow, no matter how odd, off-topic, or strange they might be.

For instance, while you are sitting in the library trying to think of something to say about climate change, the thought of going fishing keeps creeping into your mind. You could dismiss the thought as a distraction (and a temptation), but if you hold on to it you may find that the best way to talk about atmospheric CO_2 concentrations is to talk about how climate change can affect personal hobbies like fishing.

Giving Yourself Time to Invent

Whether your goal is an innovative statement, a persuasive argument, or just a new answer to an old question, giving yourself time to invent at the beginning of your project is much more efficient and less stressful than trying to develop a new idea or new perspective as the deadline nears.

MODULE II-2

INVENTION STRATEGIES

Here are step-by-step instructions for seven popular, tried-and-true invention strategies:

- freewriting
- listing
- looping
- a picture = 10,000 words
- explosive writing
- constrictive writing
- say it again and again

Different strategies will work better for different tasks. Give yourself time to practice each one and determine which ones work best for you. For most of these strategies, your first step should be to kick everyone out, shut the door, turn off all the noise, and silence your cellphone so that you can concentrate on the task at hand.

Freewriting

Freewriting is writing quickly, without stopping, for at least 500 words or two pages. When done effectively, freewriting produces the raw materials for ideas without self-monitoring or self-criticism. It is an excellent strategy for overcoming writer's block.

Step One: Set Your Task and Goals

- At the very top of the page, write your goal—to write without stopping, correcting, or editing for at least two pages.
- Write your question, subject, or issue on the next line.
- Remind yourself that you will not get up or allow yourself to be distracted until you have written 500 words.

Step Two: Write

- Write 500 words, or two pages, as fast as you can without editing, erasing, or correcting.
- If you are writing on a computer, make the screen dark so you cannot see what you are doing. Make it bright again to save your work when you are done. If you are working on paper, don't look back as you write.

- If your mind wanders, write down the wandering thought and try to link it back to your question, subject, or issue.

Step Three: Reflect and Move Forward

- Save, analyze, and select as described below in "Critiquing and Selecting at the End."

Listing

Listing requires you to write for at least 10 minutes, but you can continue for as long as it is productive to do so. It can be especially helpful at the beginning of the writing process. It is also well suited to helping you develop ideas as you write or as you confront writer's block.

Step One: Start Your List

If you are developing your own subject,

- list words or phrases that describe what it is about the subject that interests you, and
- list words or phrases that describe the steps you think you should take as you explore your subject.

If you are responding to an assignment,

- list words or phrases that describe the things you must do or talk about, and
- list words or phrases that describe what you can say or would like to say about the assigned subject.

If you are struggling with a problem,

- list all of the ways you have tried to solve the problem, and
- make a list of all the things that are keeping you from a solution.
- Then review the two lists you have just made, and make a third list of the ways in which a friend, an expert, or your professor might solve the problem.

Step Two: Reflect and Move Forward

- Save, analyze, and select as described below in "Critiquing and Selecting at the End."

Looping

Some strategies are designed to generate a subject to write about. **Looping** is a kind of mapping method that helps you explore and expand upon an assigned subject or subject you have in mind.

For example, a common assignment in many nonfiction and journalism courses is to write your own personality profile. Looping would help you map out and bundle the mishmash of experiences, memories, and events that is your life.

Step One: Center Your Question, Issue, or Subject

- At the very top of the page write down your goal—to write without stopping, correcting, erasing, or editing for at least 20 minutes.
- In the center of the page, write a word or brief phrase that represents your question, issue, or assigned subject and draw a circle around it. (See Figure 2.2.)

Figure 2.2
Typical results of a looping exercise.

Step Two: Loop

- Think about the word or phrase at the center of your page, write down the next idea that comes to your mind, and then draw a circle around it and draw a line between the first circle and the second. Continue as you think of additional words and ideas.
- As your loops multiply, you will find some of your ideas relate to the center idea and some relate to other loops. Draw lines wherever you see relationships.

- Some ideas are of another kind. If one idea is the opposite of or hostile to another, use a dotted line to express this relationship.
- Feel free to use different colored pens or pencils to express the differences and similarities between the ideas.

Step Three: Reflect and Move Forward

- Save, analyze, and select as described below in "Critiquing and Selecting at the End."

A Picture = 10,000 Words

A picture = 10,000 words draws upon thought-provoking images to help you develop a subject or an approach to a subject. It can help you to explore a complex or jumbled scene, mine a dynamic social situation for hidden meaning, or just provoke memories. Freezing the frame, as a photograph does, will help you focus on what would otherwise be a blur of activity.

Step One: Find an Image

If you have been given a subject, describe it in five words or a couple of brief phrases on the top of a blank page or screen.

If you have no subject, type three words or a short phrase that comes to mind.

- Using the words or phrase, search for three images that best represent your initial description. If you need to search for images, try databases and networks such as Pinterest, Flickr, or Picsearch.
- The images can have a theme, such as three images from a county fair, or the images can simply catch your eye, such as a scuba diver, a sunset, and a street sign. They can be positive or negative representations, they can represent the whole of your subject or parts of it, and they can even seem unrelated, but for some reason they just stick with you.
- Select your images. If they are on your phone or camera, print them large or save them and put them on a big screen.

Step Two: Write

- Study the three images and then write about them as fast as you can without stopping, correcting, erasing, or editing for at least 500 words or two pages.
- If your mind wanders, write down the wandering thought and try to link it back to your question, subject, or issue.

Step Three: Reflect and Move Forward

- Save, analyze, and select as described below in "Critiquing and Selecting at the End."

Explosive Writing

Explosive writing requires that you write for 10 minutes at least three different times during a single day. This strategy is well suited to creative-writing tasks like developing scenes, settings, and character profiles.

Step One: Light the Fuse

- Explosive writing can happen on the go; therefore, during the day you will need to carry a notebook and pens or pencils, or a mobile device you like to write on. You will also need an alarm like a cellphone alarm.
- At the very top of your paper or screen, write down your goal—when the alarm sounds, you will write without stopping, correcting, or editing for at least 10 minutes.
- Set your alarm, or some reminder, so that at least three times during the day, you will begin your explosive writing exercise.

Step Two: Write

- When the alarm goes off, stop wherever you are (if you can), take a deep breath, and look around. Look for at least two minutes, and be sure to look in all directions.
- If something catches your eye, focus on it. If nothing catches your eye, focus on the feel, mood, atmosphere, and tone of the space you are in.
- Then write one page, or around 300 words, about your focus. You can begin with a description, but end with some kind of concluding statement about what you have seen.
- Don't forget to save each entry.

Step Three: Reflect and Move Forward

- Save, analyze, and select as described below in "Critiquing and Selecting at the End."

Constrictive Writing

This strategy helps many writers and poets to improve their language skills and create surprising compositions. To use **constrictive writing**, you put an artificial limit on yourself and try to write around that limit. For example, in 1939, Ernest Vincent wrote the novel *Gadsby: A Story of Over 50,000 Words without Using the Letter "E."*

Step One: Create Your Constriction

- Don't be easy on yourself.
- Consider writing two pages composed of sentences that are all exactly five words long. Or write two pages about a subject (such as rattlesnakes) without using any words that describe or represent your subject (words like reptile, snake, slither, and coldblooded would be off-limits, for example).
- Write down your subject and your constraint or limit at the top of your page or screen.

Step Two: Write

- Unlike freewriting, constrictive writing allows you to write very slowly and thoughtfully. Don't edit what you have written, but if you want to take another crack at a sentence to make it better, feel free to try again, and again, and again.
- Do not worry about paragraph structure or internal logic. Simply say as much as you can given the constraint or limit.
- Save and set aside your work for at least two hours.

Step Three: Reflect and Move Forward

- Save, analyze, and select as described below in "Critiquing and Selecting at the End."

Say It Again and Again

The **say it again and again** strategy focuses on rewriting and helps you think about how words and ideas are constructed and how ideas develop as people discuss and trade thoughts. Writers have used this technique successfully for hundreds of years. This strategy works best with a specific subject or idea, as it helps you explore different sides of a dispute or different perspectives on a subject.

Step One: Find Your Focus

- Write a brief sentence that describes your subject at the top of the page. Or summarize your thesis or an opposing claim in a single sentence at the top of the page.

- This is not freewriting. You may write slowly and deliberatively. But try not to go back and revise or edit.

Step Two: Write

- Rewrite the subject sentence 30 times.
- You can change the sentence structure or use synonyms to recast the sentence, but your rephrased sentences cannot look or sound exactly like the first one. Also, each sentence must have roughly the same meaning as the first.
- After experimenting with **synonyms**, different words that mean the same thing (like *fast* and *quick*), you will need to look for other ways to rephrase. Try different sentence structures, shift from a positive statement to a negative one, and think about the relationships between the parts of speech (between a verb and noun, for example). For example, the lyric "we are never getting back together" can be recast as "coupling is not in our future." The two sentences are similar, but the noun and verb shift makes a big change.
- It is easy to get distracted during this exercise and lose momentum. Keep in mind that the benefits do not become apparent until after you have rephrased your sentence at least 20 times. Patience is required.

Step Three: Reflect and Move Forward

- Save, analyze, and select as described below in "Critiquing and Selecting at the End."

Critiquing and Selecting at the End

Because you won't be critiquing or editing ideas as they come to you, once you've used invention strategies to generate lots of raw material, you will have to decide how best to move forward. The following steps will help you move from invention to evaluating the ideas you have generated.

- Set aside your invention work for at least two hours, and then return to it with fresh eyes. Each invention session is an act of surprise. If you move too quickly to drafting, you will not benefit from the shift in perspective that time can provide.
- When you come back to your work after a pause, be ready to take notes or jot down new ideas as you look for links you had not considered before. Search out new approaches, perspectives, or definitions.
- Prioritize. Make a list of ideas and connections that provoke the most thought and ideas, even if they are negative or critical ideas.

- Make a list of ideas and connections that seem closest to or help you think about your assignment or your subject.
- Organize your ideas into topics. For example, in the looping exercise you might list all the ideas that bridge or link with a single, common bubble or word. Or write all the ideas on separate sticky notes, put them on a wall, and try different clusters of topics.
- Organize your ideas and connections into types:
  - ideas that explain
  - ideas that are examples
  - ideas that prove or challenge
  - ideas that redefine or shift perspective
- Start to think of the ideas and connections you have generated in terms of your assignment, your purpose, and your audience. Chapter 4 guides you through framing your ideas or subject. Chapter 3 helps you understand your audience's expectations, and Module I-3 discusses the objectives and purposes common to academic contexts.

MODULE II-3

USING RESEARCH TO FIND AND DEVELOP IDEAS

Three Reasons to Use Research to Invent

What does research do for you? Here are three reasons to invest in the process.

1. **Research provides you with data and information beyond your own experience**. Research allows you to tap into the hard work already done by thinkers, scholars, and people like yourself trying to figure out difficult problems. For example, you may have heard that Ebola is deadly and untreatable. However, without facts and data all you have is heresay. A quick review of the World Health Organization's website will provide a May 30, 2018, article documenting the successful use of a vaccine to control Ebola in the Democratic Republic of the Congo and a brief history of the development of the vaccine.
2. **Research yields data, information, and knowledge**. Research gives you an understanding of how people talk about your subject and how audiences respond to different types of arguments about your subject. You may not know what "breaking the taper on the ball joint" means if you don't hang around auto technicians. And yet a little research and reading in a "Chilton Auto Repair Manual" will not only explain what it means but also make a case for the best way to do it.

3. **Research can enhance your thinking with solid reasoning and reliable evidence, giving your argument more authority and persuasiveness**. From an audience's perspective, the only way you can persuade others about the Ebola vaccine or use terms like *ball joint taper* correctly is if you know what you are talking about. To be persuasive, you must convince your reader that you are a knowledgeable source on your topic.

Research Defined

The word **research** describes a three-step process, outlined in Figure 2.3, in which you gather and analyze information and then draw conclusions from it.

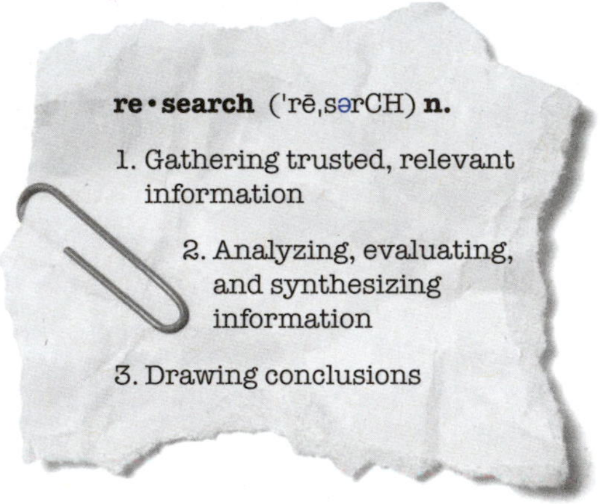

re • search (ˈrē,sərCH) **n.**

1. Gathering trusted, relevant information

2. Analyzing, evaluating, and synthesizing information

3. Drawing conclusions

Figure 2.3
The three steps in the research process.

When you conduct research, you are looking beyond your own ideas to discover what you do not know. In the same way that you look around to friends, peers, and your community to gather new ideas and different opinions, when you do research you look to scholars and experts to learn more.

This chapter demonstrates how to research, evaluate, and incorporate sources you discover. Module II-4 explains how databases and search engines work and how to use them to identify relevant information and data you can trust. Module II-6 helps you analyze, and evaluate what you have found, and Module VI-1 provides tools to avoid logical fallacies and make sure your conclusions are sound.

Research Is Invention

During the invention stage, you are not using research to prove or disprove a thesis, or to argue for or against a point of view. The initial purpose of research is to discover information that will provoke and expand your thinking. In fact, research during invention is a bit like a study-abroad program.

The goal of studying abroad is to be exposed to other cultures and perspectives, absorb a different language, and consider other ways of thinking as a means to enhance your own. Just as you need to engage in conversations to get the most from a travel experience, you need to throw yourself into the conversations about your subject to get the most from research.

Each idea, discovery, debate, opinion, and argument about a subject is part of a conversation that has been going on for some time. Research is part of your preparation to join the conversation so that when you do, your ideas will be heard and respected.

Researching to invent requires a different kind of reading from what you will do later in the process. Whether you need a clearly defined subject and approach or you already have them, the goal during invention is to read for ideas that provoke more ideas.

A trick to wringing the most provocative ideas from the research you do at this stage is to play both the believing game and the doubting game.

The Believing Game

When you play the believing game, you suspend your disbelief and put your critical impulse on hold, as you often do when you watch certain types of movies. It is easy to act like you believe in positions you agree with. The challenge and real benefit come when you play the believing game while reading or seeing strange or even disagreeable opinions and expressions. If you play the game well, the benefits of believing are significant.

1. As a research tool, the believing game keeps your eyes open. Rather than dismissing an argument you disagree with, playing the believing game will allow you to consider the points of the argument fairly.

2. If you are preparing an argument, you are often trying to persuade someone who thinks differently than you do. The believing game helps you understand your audience's point of view—what its members think and why they would disagree with you—before you make your argument.

3. The believing game also allows you to test your own argument before you go public. To do this, you need to discover your argument's weakness and anticipate counterarguments opposing your position. If you can believe in counterarguments to your own position, you will be able to anticipate points, questions, reasons, and evidence put forward by future opponents. Your audience may not have these counterarguments in mind, but if you can raise them and then deal with them in your own argument, you have a better chance of persuading your audience.

Breaking the Block
The Believing Game

For this strategy, you will adopt the perspective of the author or creator of a work. Not only must you imagine that you agree with him or her, you must also assume you want to promote the ideas and opinions you have read. Then you will expand the author's idea to see where it leads. The writing component of this exercise will take 15–20 minutes.

Remember that this game is a tool for provoking ideas so you can build persuasive arguments.

Step One: Research

Find an editorial, blog post, image, or any expression of an opinion or idea that you find disagreeable or strange.

At the very top of a blank screen or page, write your goals:

- You will read or observe the text you found.
- You will accept (for the time being) the author's perspective and claim, extend its logic, develop additional supportive reasons, and apply it in different situations.

Start reading or observing and believing.

Step Two: Write

Set your timer for 10 minutes and begin writing without stopping, correcting, or editing for at least that amount of time.

If you are struggling, use each of the lines below to start a new paragraph.

- I believe it, and it affects me…
- I believe it, and that changes my understanding of the past…
- I believe it, and so now I must rethink…
- I believe it, and so in the future…

After at least 10 minutes, write one more paragraph in which you describe the beliefs, values, and thinking of someone who holds the position you just tried to believe.

Step Three: Reflect
Set your work aside for at least two hours.

When you come back to it, look for ideas, lines of thought, or questions that can help you develop your own ideas and perhaps find your subject.

The Doubting Game

The doubting game is a critical approach. Rather than trying to adopt the author's perspective, as in the believing game, you pull back from it and try to identify errors, problems in reasoning, and negative or unforeseen implications that will undermine the argument.

The doubting game can help you understand your own positions more clearly and refine your thinking on a given issue. It is most useful during invention as a way of provoking a "**rebound response**." For example, you may never have given space exploration much thought until someone close to you mentions that she is studying engineering because she wants to be an astronaut and go to Mars. Listening, you might begin to think of arguments against investing in or even thinking about space travel. Without your friend's comments to react to, however, you would never have built an argument against space travel.

Figure 2.4
René Descartes doubted everything he could not prove, leaving one truth: "I think; therefore I am."

Breaking the Block
The Doubting Game

Examine a brief argument and then build a case against it. The writing component of this exercise will take 15–20 minutes.

Step One: Research

Find a brief journalistic editorial, preferably about an issue in which you have no interest at all. If you have been given an assignment, look for an editorial that takes a position on the assigned issue.

At the top of a blank screen or page, write your goals:

- You will read the editorial once.
- Then you will read through it slowly one more time and underline each individual assertion and each bit of supporting evidence.

Step Two: Write

Start at the beginning of the editorial and write for 10 minutes. For each paragraph of the editorial, write a sentence describing the error, fault, or contradiction you see in the argument. The following tips will help you find fault with and critique what you read.

- Doubt each point and statement.
- Look for contradictions between statements, assumptions the writer is making (for example, that the taxpaying public should approve of how tax money is spent), and parts of the argument.
- Examine the editorial for errors in logic, such as assumptions that will not hold and exaggerations.
- Think of evidence and reasons that would refute the central argument.
- Consider negative consequences if the argument won the day or the proposal were adopted.

Step Three: Reflect

Set your work aside for at least two hours.

When you come back to it, try to string your marginal notes together in the form of a rough outline. As you do, imagine you are writing to the same audience as the author you just critiqued.

MODULE II-4

USING DATABASES AND SEARCH ENGINES

Just as when you consult a map, when you use a search engine you must first have a destination or subject in mind. Even a vague one will do at first. When you have an idea, it is time to ask yourself this very basic question: Where does the knowledge I need live?

Deciding Where the Knowledge You Need Lives

Most of us would have little trouble finding departure times for May 4 flights from Boston to Austin; we would visit an airline website. Similarly, most of us would have no difficulty at all finding a gallon of milk in our hometown. In both cases, we know what we need and where it lives. Asking "where do political science data, information, and knowledge live?" may seem odd, but it is the first step of focused research.

Focus on the location. If you have an assignment to compare the ideas of the political scientists Aaron Wildavsky and Alan Wolfe, Google's scope may be far too large and may not provide the focus you need. So narrow your scope. Just as milk is in a dairy case in the back of the store and Kansas City lives on the Kansas–Missouri border, political science scholarship lives in a few specific databases and collections.

To focus within your scope, find out where scholars of your subject keep their ideas, writing, and documents. There are a number of ways to do this, but here are three easy methods:

1. Ask your professor.
2. Ask a reference librarian.
3. Consult the Library of Congress (LOC) subject-heading list.

The Library of Congress classification system assigns a unique call number to each item in the collection. Each call number starts with a letter or sequence of letters. Each letter stands for a general subject area. For example, the LOC assigns the subject of political science the call letter "J." If you look within "J," you will find Aaron Wildavsky's books in the subsection JK which holds documents about US political institutions and public administration (Figure 2.5). You will also find academic journals in the field of political science. To see the entire LOC subject-heading list, including subsections such as JK, follow this link to the Library of Congress Classification Outline: http://www.loc.gov/catdir/cpso/lcco/.

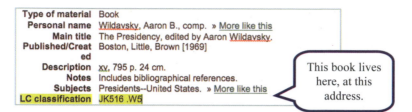

Type of material	Book
Personal name	Wildavsky, Aaron B., comp. » More like this
Main title	The Presidency, edited by Aaron Wildavsky.
Published/Created	Boston, Little, Brown [1969]
Description	xv, 795 p. 24 cm.
Notes	Includes bibliographical references.
Subjects	Presidents--United States. » More like this
LC classification	JK516 .W5

This book lives here, at this address.

Figure 2.5 The Library of Congress classification number for this book will be the same in every library that uses the LOC.

Breaking the Block
Parachute In to Discover a Topic

Developing your own subject for a paper or presentation may seem daunting, especially if you are in a course that is already disorienting or overwhelming. Do not worry. You probably discovered many of your interests by chance, and you can become interested in unfamiliar subjects as well. Sometimes researchers can force such happy accidents simply by jumping in and seeing where they land. This exercise is a useful way to discover writing topics within specific subject areas. You will need to spend some time in the library.

Step One: Prepare Your Work Space

- Grab a laptop or iPad or two pens or pencils and a legal pad.
- In the library, find the Library of Congress classification outline: the subject list used to organize books and journals.
- If you can't locate it easily, ask a librarian or look it up online: http://www.loc.gov/catdir/cpso/lcco/.
- Choose a subject that interests you (for example, forestry, English, sports, music). Look for the shelves that hold books on this subject and wander from the beginning to the end. Then locate the periodicals on this subject, which may be shelved in a different location.
- Pull three books, journals, or magazines from the shelves, find a desk, and sit down.
- Turn to the table of contents and choose a place to start reading, or flip open the publication at random. Read each one for 10 minutes.

Step Two: Write

- After reading and reviewing, make a list of ideas that caught your eye, that interested you, or that you disagree with.

- Choose one of the ideas from your list and write down your thoughts about the idea as fast as you can for 10 minutes.
- Keep in mind that the best reading notes are usually questions. For example, if you read that Aaron Wildavsky argued that once in office presidents are always drawn to foreign policy over domestic policy, you might ask, "Is that a bad thing?" "What makes Wildavsky think so?" "Is this also true of presidents who had little experience with foreign policy before being elected?"
- Set aside your work for at least two hours. Before you pick it up again, review your assignment and what is expected of you.
- When you review your 10-minute writing, look to see how close your thoughts are to the expectations for the assignment.
- If you see connections, discuss your initial thoughts with your professor or with classmates who can help you evaluate and develop your ideas for the assignment.

There are many paths to the knowledge you need. If you have an assigned topic, zero in on your subject area. But keep in mind that Google and a library catalogue or an Online Public Access Catalog (OPAC) are not the only paths to tracking down the knowledge you need. Academic databases, and their associated search engines, are a fast, efficient path into disciplines and the information that lives there.

Search your library's homepage for databases. You will likely find a link to an alphabetical list or a subject index of available databases. Using the subject index, you will commonly find a number of databases specializing in various disciplines. For example, you can find political science scholarship such as *Worldwide Political Science Abstracts* or the *CQ Press Voting and Elections Collection*. You can also use the "advanced search" function of database search engines such as JSTOR and ProQuest to focus your search on the subject of political science.

Use subject headings to search databases. It is not possible for database managers to anticipate every word a researcher might use to describe a subject. However, most search engines linked to specialized databases and collections use a limited subject-heading list. Sometimes a search engine will offer suggested subject headings as you type in the search box. Sometimes databases will list their subject headings as a drop-down menu. The American Economic Association database has the drop-down menu shown in Figure 2.6.

Search By Phrase: ⊙ Search By Keywords: ○

Categories selected to search in:

☑ Title
☑ Abstract
☑ Author (Last name)

Filter by JEL Classification.

✓ All JEL classifications
  A – General Economics and Teaching
  B – History of Economic Thought, Methodology, and...
  C – Mathematical and Quantitative Methods
  D – Microeconomics
  E – Macroeconomics and Monetary Economics
  F – International Economics
  G – Financial Economics
  H – Public Economics
  I – Health, Education, and Welfare
  J – Labor and Demographic Economics
  K – Law and Economics
  L – Industrial Organization
  M – Business Administration and Business Economics...
  N – Economic History
  O – Economic Development, Technological Change, and...
  P – Economic Systems
  Q – Agricultural and Natural Resource Economics...
  R – Regional, Real Estate, and Transportation Economics
  Y – Miscellaneous Categories
  Z – Other Special Topics

Figure 2.6
An example
of a drop-
down menu
of specialized
search terms.

Google Scholar allows you to search for articles in journals with specific subjects. Click on the three bars in the upper left corner of Google Scholar. This will open up an advanced search box (Figure 2.7). There you will find a box with the phrase "Return articles **published** in." In this box, you can use the LOC subject headings (see above) to find articles and books within a specific subject or specialty.

Find articles   ✕

with **all** of the words   _____

with the **exact phrase**   _____

with **at least one** of the words _____

without the words   _____

where my words occur   [anywhere in the article ⇕]

Return articles **authored by**   _____
                                   e.g., "PJ Hayes" or McCarthy

Return articles **published in**   _____
                                   e.g., J Biol Chem or Nature

Return articles **dated between** [____] — [____]
                                   e.g., 1996

[🔍]

Figure 2.7 The advanced search function in Google Scholar.

Using Tricks of the Trade to Find the Knowledge You Need

As you can imagine, there are tricks of the research trade that yield the most relevant results, or hits, in the least amount of time with the least effort. A **hit** is the information about a source such as an article or a book that a search engine returns on a results page. Here are a few strategies to find what you need efficiently.

Ask an expert for help. In research there are two kinds of experts, librarians and those who have already researched and written about your subject. You can tap the expertise of both.

Major libraries will have reference librarians who specialize in various disciplines, and small libraries are staffed by librarians who are thoroughly familiar with the tools and resources available. If you have a subject, a librarian will point you to the databases and catalogue subject headings that will be most productive.

If a scholar has done the research necessary to write an article or book and a reputable publisher or journal has published it, odds are that the sources that author used are authoritative. Bibliographies and "works cited" pages are an excellent way to focus and enhance your research. In addition, the sources you read can lead you to additional sources as they are likely to have relied on sources as well.

Learn search-engine tricks. Most search engines use set theory to translate the words or phrase you type into commands the computer can understand. You do not need to learn set theory, but you should learn the tricks that allow you to search precisely and efficiently.

If you use "and" to separate your search terms, a search engine will bring back only documents that have both words.

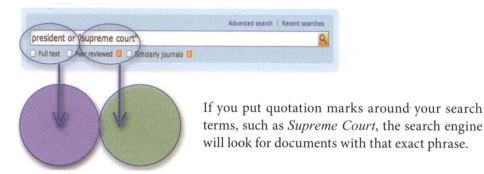

If you put quotation marks around your search terms, such as *Supreme Court*, the search engine will look for documents with that exact phrase.

If you place "or" between your search terms, your hits will include a set of documents that have the word *president*, and a set that include the phrase *Supreme Court*.

Placing the word "not" in front of a search term or phrase will exclude all documents that have the term or phrase from the hits returned.

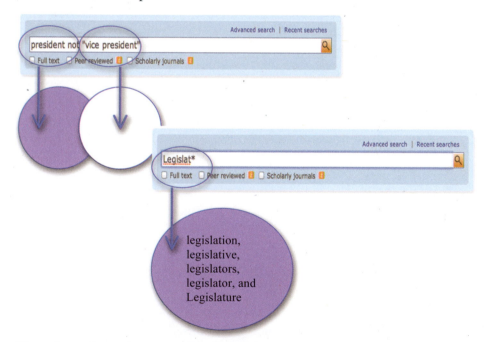

If you do not know how to spell a word, don't know how it begins or ends, or if you want to find documents that include all variations of a word, place a "*" at the front or end of your search term. As the example above shows, a search of "Legislat*" will bring back documents that include the words *legislation, legislative, legislators, legislator,* and *Legislature*.

Each search engine is a little different, but most offer tips in the support or help pages.

Use keyword combinations. The goal of any search is to return the most relevant, most useful, and most authoritative hits. If your search returns thousands of hits, the scope is too large. If your search returns fewer than three hits, and these hits are not helpful, it is too tightly focused.

Ideally, you want as many hits as you can reasonably review and evaluate. To make a precise search, you need to search within a subject and use keywords to zero in on specific information. A **keyword** is a significant word used to index or reference information.

When you are doing research to gather or develop your ideas during the early stages of writing, prepare and use a brief list of keywords in different combinations. For example, if you are interested in the qualities of our most effective presidents, typing "effective AND president" into a search box will bring up an overwhelming number of hits.

Instead, first create a list of potential search words. Then do a series of searches using different combinations of *three* of these terms. A student searching within the subject of political science might try the following strings of keywords linked by "and":

1. President   Leadership   Qualities
2. President   Excellent   Vision

As you search in this way, you are likely to discover very long and very brief lists of entries. If your list has more than 100 entries, a different, more focused, list of keywords will help you narrow down your results. Whenever you discover a manageable list of entries, save your hit list and highlight the search terms used to generate each hit list. Module II-6 will give you the tools to evaluate the sources on your hit list.

MODULE II-5

ORGANIZING YOUR RESEARCH

Excellent research is part searching and part record keeping. The best, most exhaustive research plan and schedule are of little value if you cannot retrieve and use the data, information, and documents you discovered during research. Your research will yield a treasure trove of great ideas, and you must be able to record them as you discover them.

Over time, successful students, professional researchers, and scholars have developed tricks of the trade that make researching, organizing findings, and integrating sources easier and quicker.

- **Search, retrieve, and then read**. You should first search for data, information, and documents, and then review and read your discoveries, keeping the two activities separate. Resist the temptation to stop and read an article you have found while doing your initial search.
- **Keep track of your search history**. Repeating a search you have already done is time consuming. Most database search engines allow you to export your search history and the hits for each search. If not, print out or save each search results page, and mark each search with the terms you used to find the results.
- **Get hard copies, or complete electronic copies**. If you download an article from a database, make sure your copy includes all the documentation information you will need to write a works-cited or references entry or a bibliography. Chapter 7 details the essential information you will need.
- **Take notes in the same way and same place**. Hard copies make it easy to take notes on the data set or document as you read. Note taking on electronic documents, however, allows you to search your notes with your computer's search function.

  Your notes should include the following information:
  - all of the information needed to document the source.
  - the quotation, paraphrase, or summary you find relevant.
  - the page number of the quotation, paraphrase, or summary.
  - your thoughts, such as why you found the source important and relevant to your argument.
- **Keep a Dialectical Notebook**. While you are reviewing and reading your research, you are engaged in a conversation. Ideas will flow as they do in a real conversation. To keep track of the ideas and information you discover and the questions they inspire in your thinking, jot down your thoughts as you read. A **dialectal notebook** (Figure 2.8) makes it easy. On a blank page, draw a line down the center or create two columns on your screen. On the left side, write or type in quotations, summaries, and paraphrases from the source you are reading. Don't forget to include page numbers. On the right side, write down the questions and insights that occur to you. Often, these notes will become paragraphs in your final paper.

> LeFevre, Karen Burke. *Invention as a Social Act*. Southern Illinois UP, 1987.
>
> "If we take a rhetorical view of the entire process of invention instead of focusing on the production of a text, we may be more inclined to regard talking and acting as part of the process, as surely they should be." (page 31)
>
> I think she is right and I wonder why universities and disciplines outside of English don't study how people come up with ideas.

Figure 2.8 Dialectical notes record your conversation with the text.

- **Keep all your research, notes, and drafts together**. If you cannot pick up a single bag or box or open a single electronic folder that holds all your work on a project or assignment, you risk losing important work. Keep everything in one place so that you will not misplace or overlook anything. That does not mean having only one copy, however. Read on.
- **Maintain three points of contact**. As climbers move up a rock face, they try to maintain three points of contact, three holds, in order to hang on. Likewise, you need to have three points of contact for your research notes and drafts, such as your laptop hard drive or a thumb drive, a print copy, and a file on a cloud storage service such as Dropbox or Google Drive. Having three copies of your research files on the same computer gives you only one point of contact; lose or crash your computer and you lose your research.
- **Save different versions of your research notes and drafts**. Each time you add a note or citation or make even a small revision on a draft, save it as a different version of the same document. You can identify each version by adding the current date to the file name, or you can simply add a number each time you save:

    Dropbox/History 404/ResearchNotes 4
    Dropbox/History 404/ResearchNotes 5

- **Use Track Changes**. Any time you add to or edit your notes, turn on the Track Changes option. By doing so, you will build a record of your thoughts as they evolve, and you will be able to recover cuts you might later regret. In addition, many portfolio-based assignments ask you to draft a reflection essay describing the development of a project. If you do not track your changes, you will have to rely on your memory to recall them.

- **Mark the words, work, and ideas of others**. If you cut and paste *anything* from *any* source onto a different page or file, highlight the excerpt in a distinct color and place quotation marks around the entire excerpt. If you have summarized or paraphrased a source, use a different color to highlight the text so you will remember to document the source. This way, as your research notes become the draft of your argument, you will know what ideas are yours and what ideas must be cited.

Research Checklist

The checklist below can serve as a reminder of the tricks of the research trade. Copy it and keep it in your notebook or near your computer.

Research Checklist

1. Learn where the information you need lives.

2. Use the database and search engine that best fit your subject and needs.

3. Search within your subject. Use subject headings to limit searches.

4. Search precisely using search-engine tricks.

5. Make a list of promising key terms and try them in different combinations.

6. Keep track of your search history.

7. Search for, retrieve, and then read the information you have discovered.

MODULE II-6

HOW DO I EVALUATE SOURCES?

If you base your evaluation of sources only on the message and how it fits your argument, you are likely to incorporate some questionable opinions and information, and you may make the serious mistake of discarding credible arguments and evidence simply because they do not agree with your thesis. Thus, before you can incorporate sources that support your thesis or deal with those that argue against you, you must evaluate the sources you have discovered.

Responsible Sourcing
How to Evaluate Your Sources

To evaluate your sources, look at each source from three different perspectives:

1. The origin, author, publisher, or container of the source.
2. The elements or components of the source, such as the genre and documentation.
3. The message of the source.

Each perspective in turn allows you to apply three different criteria, or measures, to evaluate the source:

A. Honesty
B. Authority
C. Relevance

Combining the perspectives and the criteria, the three steps of each source evaluation look like this:

1. Where did the source come from, or what is known about its author, publisher, or container?

 A. Is the origin honest? Is the author identified and known? Do you recognize the site or container?
 B. Is the origin of the source authoritative? What makes the author or publisher an expert or reliable?
 C. Is the origin of the source relevant to my argument and my audience?

2. What is the source, or what is known about its genre, documentation, or other elements?

A. Is the source constructed honestly? How is the information verified? Are quotations complete, clipped, or taken out of context?
B. Are the markers of authority valid and will my audience recognize them? Is the construction like other authoritative texts of the same type?
C. Is the type or kind of source relevant to my argument and my audience?

3. What is the message of the source?

A. Will my audience find the argument or expression honest? Does this information appeal to fears or confirm unfounded biases or beliefs?
B. Will my audience find the argument or expression authoritative? Is the source simply opinion or supported by verifiable information?
C. Is the argument or expression relevant to my argument and my audience?

As the "Responsible Sourcing" box indicates, you need to apply the criteria of relevance, authority, and honesty to each source you consider. Remember, the goal of a public argument is not to persuade yourself or signal your beliefs to those who think as you do. Academic arguments are built of honest, authoritative, and relevant findings to persuade an audience that thinks, believes, and acts differently than you do.

MODULE II-7

AVOIDING PLAGIARISM

To avoid plagiarism, you need to know what causes it, how to accurately cite your sources, and how to fairly reproduce or represent the work, language, or ideas you are using.

Understanding Its Causes

It is impossible to list all the causes and motivations that lead to an act of plagiarism. However, there are a few recurring situations that contribute to plagiarism.

First, intentional plagiarism usually happens the night before a paper is due. At 4:00 a.m., a desperate student will find information, paragraphs, and even complete papers that can be downloaded, disguised, and handed in the next morning. Second, the pressure to turn something in, especially if you have never missed a deadline, can overwhelm your better judgment. This explains why most students found plagiarizing are usually capable people who have never plagiarized before but were worried the professor would think them lazy or incapable if they did not turn in a paper on time.

The third cause of plagiarism is a disregard for or misunderstanding of academic conventions. It is not uncommon to discover a plagiarized paper that also contains significant research. If the writer had only taken the time to identify and integrate source material and document it according to the expected conventions, the result would have been a strong research paper. Finally, some students simply refuse to do the work. Such students are probably not reading this book. Still, it is worth pointing out that higher education is about mastering material *and* developing abilities and competencies like good work habits and disciplined concentration. In college, plagiarism can lead to a failed class. After college, it can lead to much worse. In 2019, Penn State issued a policy allowing the University to revoke degrees due to plagiarism or research misconduct. See policy at https://almanac.upenn.edu/articles/of-record-policy-on-revocation-of-degrees. Many colleges and universities now have similar policies.

Now you know the situations you should avoid. Next, what *should* you do? What steps will help you actively avoid plagiarism?

Knowing What to Cite

Responsible sourcing is not difficult. You need to know what you must cite and what you do not have to cite. You need to keep track of what you have discovered. And you need to be sure that your reader knows what data, information, and ideas came from which sources, and make clear which ideas are your own.

You *do* need to cite any source you quote directly, but also any work, language, or ideas that you use in summaries or paraphrases or as images. Even if you only mention or reference an idea, you must cite it.

You do not have to cite common knowledge. **Common knowledge** includes the following:

- **well known** data, information, and ideas such as that Notre Dame is a Catholic university;
- data, information, and ideas **commonly known by the audience** you intend to persuade, for example the fact that Notre Dame students know that their kilt-wearing cheerleaders are called the Irish Guard;
- **widely available and not controversial** data, information, and ideas such as the fact that the artist Millard Sheets created the mural often referred to as "Touchdown Jesus" on the Notre Dame campus.

However, if your research leads you to assert that the modernist style of the Touchdown Jesus mural was a response to the reforms of the second Vatican Council, this assertion is not common knowledge. Therefore, you need to quote, summarize, or paraphrase this information and cite the article that informed your opinion.

If you are not sure if the information you want to use is common knowledge, play it safe. Document any information that may be questioned by or unknown to a reasonable member of your audience.

Responsible Sourcing
Track Sources during Research

Often, plagiarism happens because students simply lose track of who said what in their research notes. You need to mark ideas that came from your research so you know what to cite. Here are some tricks used by professional researchers and writers to help you keep track of the ideas you discover during research.

- During the initial stages of research, whether you work on screen or on paper, make sure the source material is visibly distinct from your own writing. Use highlighting, bold, or italics. For example, highlight in yellow every phrase, line, or paragraph you copy from a source. Highlight in orange any summary or paraphrase you write based on what you read in a source. Visual cues such as highlighting will remind you of what you need to cite.
- As you integrate source material into your own writing, first add the citation to the "Works Cited," "References," or "Bibliography" page. Then place the quotation, paraphrase, or summary in your text (Module II-8 shows you how to use quotations and to write paraphrases and summaries). Be sure to use quotation marks when you use the source's exact words and include page numbers and other in-text information required of the documentation style you are using.
- Finally, make sure each quotation, paraphrase, and summary is paired with its full citation on the "Works Cited," "References," or "Bibliography" page. After you double-check each source and citation, remove the highlighting, bold type, or italics you used to differentiate source material. Chapter 7 will help you understand how citations work.

MODULE II-8

INTEGRATING SOURCES AUTHORITATIVELY

Thorough research will yield pages of notes and documentation information, as well as pages of the work, language, and ideas of others copied from the sources you have read and researched. Since you cannot use it all, you have to think about how to use the sources fairly and persuasively.

There are four common ways of using sources within the body of your argument: (1) brief quotations, (2) lengthy block quotations, (3) paraphrases, and (4) summaries.

These four methods of integrating sources are explained below. In addition, it's important to know how and when to use each method in order to achieve your purpose and persuade your audience. Finally, it's also important to integrate your sources into your argument smoothly.

Using Brief Quotations

A **quotation** is a phrase, sentence, or passage taken from an original source and reproduced word for word. Quotations are used for any of the following reasons:

- Your audience must see and understand the exact wording of the original.
- You are analyzing the wording, phrasing, or meaning of the original.
- The words of the original source are significantly distinct or so profoundly constructed that a summary or paraphrase would alter the meaning.
- You want to emphasize a point made by the author or emphasize the relationship of the author and her or his words.

Enclose a quotation in quotation marks and do not indent it or set it off from the text unless it is longer than four lines (MLA style) or more than forty words (APA style). In the excerpt shown in Figure 2.9, the brief quotation is marked in bold.

You may abbreviate or shorten a quotation as long as you do not change the intent or meaning of the words you use as it was commonly understood in its original context. To abbreviate a long quotation, use three periods to make an **ellipsis** (...) marking where text has been left out of a quotation.

Different documentary style manuals have different rules for ellipses. For example, if you are using MLA style and you want to cut text from the end of a quotation, you still use three periods to make an ellipsis; however, you must also include the original period, or question mark or exclamation mark, that ends the sentence. In Figure 2.10, you can see two different ellipses indicating text cut from the long block quotation. The first occurs in the middle of a sentence and the second occurs at the end followed by the period that ends the sentence.

Brackets [ ] are used to insert essential information that may be missing from a quotation because it has been abbreviated or because contextual information is absent, as in the underlined part of Figure 2.9.

For example, Bradford describes the skill and courage of one member of the ship's crew during the initial attempt to find safe harbor during the storm: **"So he [the seaman steering] bid them be of good cheer and row lustily, for there was a fair sound before them, and he doubted not but they should find one place or other where they might ride in safety"** (72).

Figure 2.9
The sentence before the quotation included the phrase "a lusty seaman which steered." Without the bracketed information, the reader would be confused.

Using Block Quotations

A **block quotation** is typically more than four lines (MLA style) or more than forty words (APA style). Block quotations should be used even more sparingly than brief quotations. Use a block quotation for any of the following reasons:

- Your audience must see and understand the exact wording of a large part of the original.
- You are analyzing the wording, meaning, or argument of a large part of the original.
- The words of the author or original source are so significantly distinct or profoundly constructed that a brief quotation would not capture these qualities of the original, and a summary or paraphrase would alter the meaning.
- You want to highlight an argument or multiple points made by the author or emphasize the relationship of the author and his or her argument.

Block quotations get their name because the entire block of quoted text is indented from the left margin. Check your documentation style manual for the depth of the indentation and for proper line spacing. The block quotation is indented, rather than enclosed in quotation marks, because a reader moving through such a large excerpt is apt to lose track of the beginning and end of the quotation and confuse the source with the surrounding text.

Too many quotations, quotations that are too long, and quotations that seem irrelevant can look like padding or filler to a professor. Be sure you link each quotation to your argument with an appropriate verb so the reason you have included it is clear. And check with your professor before using block quotations longer than half a page.

Even the mythical landing of the Pilgrims on Plymouth Rock is affected by shipwreck and is cast as a moment of destiny. What carried the first of the Pilgrims to Plymouth Rock was not the Mayflower but one of her small boats, a shallop. This shallop, tossed about by wind and waves, landed where it did purely out of the necessity to salvage life and limb from shipwreck. Bradford writes:

> The wind increased and the sea became very rough, and they broke their rudder, and it was as much as two men could do to steer her with a couple of oars . . . the storm increasing, and night drawing on, they bore what sail they could to get in, while they could see. But herewith they broke their mast in three pieces and their sail fell overboard in a very grown sea, as they had like to have been cast away. **Yet by God's mercy they recovered themselves . . . .** And though it was very dark and rained sore, in the end they got under the lee of a small island and remained there all that night in safety. (71)

Later, the small group of men **"sounded the harbor and found it fit for shipping, and marched into the land and found . . . a place (as they supposed) fit for situation"** (72).

Two things from these passages are important. For one, as the historian Samuel Eliot Morison reminds us, the anticlimactic sounding of the harbor and the weary hike on land is the only contemporary account of the landing of the Pilgrims on Plymouth Rock (Bradford 72). It is clear from the narrative that the Mayflower did not make the landing, for it was sill anchored in what is now Provincetown Harbor. . . .

Second, the Pilgrims appear to land where they did because fate drew them there, and once again, shipwreck is involved in their tale.

Works Cited

Bradford, William. *Of Plimouth Plantation, 1620-1647*. Edited by Samuel Eliot Morison, Alfred A. Knopf, 1966.

Figure 2.10
A sample page from a student's paper showing a block quotation and an in-text quotation.

MLA and APA place the in-text parenthetical citation after the block quotation punctuation (after the period).

For a quotation appearing within the text, MLA and APA place the in-text parenthetical citation before the period.

Summaries (and paraphrases) must point to a full citation (parenthetical citation before the period).

Using Paraphrases

A **paraphrase** is a detailed rewrite of a part of an original source in your own words. Use a paraphrase for any of the following reasons:

- To help your audience understand a source that uses words that are specialized, outdated, or simply unfamiliar.
- To help your audience understand a source that is highly technical or extremely detailed.
- To help your audience understand ideas or concepts that are confusing or less than clear in the original source.
- To help your audience focus on an aspect or feature of an idea found in a source.

A paraphrase typically is about as long as, and sometimes slightly longer than, the original source. A paraphrase must accurately represent the data, information, and ideas of the original without adding comments, opinions, or bias that were not in the original source. A paraphrase must be expressed in your own words and manner of expression expected by the audience. Mimicking the sentence structure of the original or using too many distinctive words from the original may be considered plagiarism.

Original	Paraphrase
The wind increased and the sea became very rough, and they broke their rudder, and it was as much as two men could do to steer her with a couple of oars . . . the storm increasing, and night drawing on, they bore what sail they could to get in, while they could see. But herewith they broke their mast in three pieces and their sail fell overboard in a very grown sea, as they had like to have been cast away.	Bradford recounts that because the rudder broke in high winds and rough seas, two men in the boat struggled to steer using oars. The people in the boat tried to make landfall under sail, but the increasingly stormy sea made progress difficult. Then, the mast broke, dropping the sail overboard, and endangering all onboard (71).

Figure 21.4

Figure 2.11
A sample paraphrase.

In the left box of Figure 2.11 is the paragraph written by William Bradford that is used as part of the block quotation. In the box on the right is a paraphrase of the Bradford paragraph. You will note that the paraphrase does not replicate Bradford's style or tone but is in the paraphraser's own words and sentence structure. It accurately represents the ideas in the original. By contrast, a faulty paraphrase of this passage might look like the one shown in Figure 2.12.

Figure 2.12
A faulty paraphrase of the passage in Figure 2.11.

The sentence structure of the paraphrase too closely mimics the original.

The order of events in the original is confused by the paraphrase (the mast broke and then they put up sail).

The writer shares an opinion not in the original.

The paraphrase uses too many of the distinctive terms of the original.

The wind got stronger and the seas rougher, and they broke their rudder, and herewith the mast broke which must have been very scary, and the sail fell overboard. Two men had to steer with a couple of oars, which was hard. The storm got worse and nightfall was coming, and so they put up as much sail as they could as they did not like to be cast away (71).

Using Summaries

A **summary** is a significant reduction of a large part of a source to its main points and ideas in your own words. Similar to a paraphrase, a summary must accurately represent the data, information, and ideas of the original without adding comments, opinions, or indications of bias that were not in the original source. You would use a summary for the following reasons:

- To help your reader understand complex ideas, a multi-point argument, or a passage that is less than clear in the original source.
- To help your reader understand and focus on the gist, or central point, of a complex idea or argument.
- To help your reader quickly connect ideas or arguments that may be spread out in long text.
- To help your reader move through your argument quickly and smoothly, with brief summaries in your own words as opposed to large block quotations of another's voice and a different manner of speaking.

In the boxed excerpt in Figure 2.13, a page-long paragraph of seventeenth-century English is summarized in two brief, easy-to-read sentences. A summary must accurately represent the original. However, you may leave out points and ideas if they are not essential to the meaning of the original and not relevant to your argument. As you read the examples of an appropriate and an inappropriate summary in Figures 2.13 and 2.14, keep in mind that the student is arguing that shipwrecks have shaped much of our understanding of America's founding.

Original	Summary
The wind increased and the sea became very rough, and they broke their rudder, and it was as much as two men could do to steer her with a couple of oars . . . the storm increasing, and night drawing on, they bore what sail they could to get in, while they could see. But herewith they broke their mast in three pieces and their sail fell overboard in a very grown sea, as they had like to have been cast away. Yet by God's mercy they recovered themselves. . . . And though it was very dark and rained sore, in the end they got under the lee of a small island and remained there all that night in safety.	Bradford describes a difficult voyage that nearly ended in shipwreck for the passengers of the boat that suffered a broken rudder and broken mast. However, all aboard survived the night protected somewhat from the storm by a small island (71).

Figure 2.13
An effective summary.

A poor summary can look like a poor paraphrase if it is too long and mimics the wording and sentence structure of the original. Or, a poor summary can look like the example in Figure 2.14. The example in Figure 2.14 is a summary of the weather conditions, but it is not a good summary of the main points of the Bradford excerpt.

Bradford recounts that the storm and wind increased and it began to get dark, but luckily a small island provided protection from the wind but not the rain (71).

Figure 2.14
An ineffective summary focusing on information that is irrelevant to the main point of the original.

A good summary is an accurate representation of the original. It represents the data, information, and ideas in the original without bias, and it does not include any opinions that were not in the original.

Choosing Quotations, Paraphrases, or Summaries

Each of the methods of incorporating sources has its own benefits, and each is used for different reasons. For example, quotations provide a sense of the quoted author's voice, tone, and language in a way that summaries cannot. On the other hand, a summary can help a reader quickly process an idea that was developed at length in the original source. To choose the best way of integrating your source, consider how the source can best support the point you are trying to make.

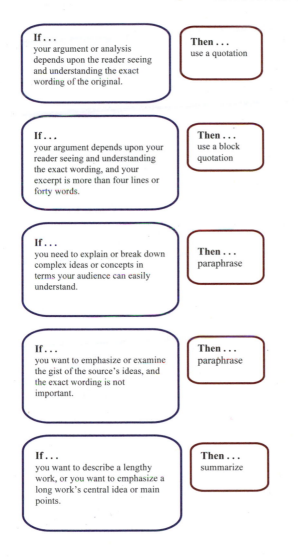

If . . .
your argument or analysis depends upon the reader seeing and understanding the exact wording of the original.

Then . . .
use a quotation

If . . .
your argument depends upon your reader seeing and understanding the exact wording, and your excerpt is more than four lines or forty words.

Then . . .
use a block quotation

If . . .
you need to explain or break down complex ideas or concepts in terms your audience can easily understand.

Then . . .
paraphrase

If . . .
you want to emphasize or examine the gist of the source's ideas, and the exact wording is not important.

Then . . .
paraphrase

If . . .
you want to describe a lengthy work, or you want to emphasize a long work's central idea or main points.

Then . . .
summarize

Keep in mind that the purpose of using sources is to support your argument. However, altering or misrepresenting a source not only robs your argument of persuasive power, but can also turn your reader against you and may result in charges of plagiarism. If you are not sure you are representing a source fairly or wonder if your interpretation of a source is accurate, visit your professor with the original source in hand and explain how you hope to use it.

Responsible Sourcing
Using Images and Sound

Using non-textual source material such as images and sounds is similar to quoting or summarizing a sentence or paragraph. Non-textual sources must be cited. In addition, there are three ways of quoting images and sounds.

1. When you reproduce an image or sound, you are trying to provide the most accurate representation of the original. A reproduced image or sound is similar to a block quotation of text. Reproducing an accurate, detailed image or sound allows you to examine the entirety of a work in detail and allows your audience to examine the parts and the whole of the work as your argument or analysis progresses. When you reproduce an image or sound, try to use the highest quality image or sound sample available.

2. You highlight a part of an image or sound to focus your audience's attention on one element or aspect. A highlight is similar to a quotation. A highlighted use does not necessarily reproduce a large portion or the entirety of an image or sound, but presents merely part of the original. When you highlight an element of a large work or sound, be sure to introduce the source, indicate it is part of a larger work or sound, and give your audience the necessary background or context for understanding the highlighted excerpt.

3. You reference, or name, an image or sound when you merely want to draw attention to its existence or its relationship to other concepts or ideas. Similar to a summary or paraphrase, when you reference, a detailed reproduction is unnecessary.

Integrating Sources

When you have spent a great deal of time writing and building your argument, it is easy for you to see the connections between your thesis and the support provided by your sources. Your audience, however, is encountering your argument and your sources for the first time and may read your work only once. What is obvious to you is what you must try to make obvious to your audience. It is up to you to explain the significance of the sources you choose.

When you bring scholars and experts into your argument, you need to do three things:

- introduce the new voice,
- let the expert speak, and
- blend her or his words with your argument.

You choose your sources based on their authority, honesty, and relevance to your argument and your audience (see Module II-6 for tips on evaluating potential sources). Having done that, you can introduce the source into your argument by explaining the following:

- **Who the source is and what their credentials are**: the name of the author and what authorizes the source as an expert and ensures her intellectual integrity. You may need to include the relevant degrees, specialties, accomplishments, publications, or offices held by the source. Scholars and experts with a great many publications have more authority than those with few publications. In addition, providing context—such as the title of the book, article, or speech from which the material comes—will help your reader understand who the source is. Remember that authority, like persuasion, happens in the mind of your audience. Research your readers' expectations and whom they respect and listen to.
- **How the source is related to your argument.** You need to help your readers understand how the source supports or contributes to your argument. This may mean breaking down or explaining a complex idea presented in the source, analyzing the information provided by the source, or synthesizing the ideas in the source with your own ideas. Before you explain, analyze, or synthesize, make sure your reader knows who is talking, why, and how the source is related to your argument, as well as what is coming.

Signal words and phrases link a source with the writer's argument. Think of signal words and phrases as road signs that alert your reader to what is next, how the next voice is related to your argument, and where the next voice is going. In the following example, a student introduces a source and signals how the reader should understand the source:

In their article "Pursuing Happiness: The Architecture of Sustainable Change," Lyubomirsky, Sheldon, and Schkade **describe** the factors that determine happiness, as seen in the pie chart in Figure 1.

Sources can support your argument in many ways including the following:

- supporting your position
  - asserts, claims, comments, concurs, confirms, goes further, ⊢ signal words
    suggests
- conceding or granting a contrary point
  - agrees, accepts, acknowledges, allows, concedes, grants, permits
- denying or disputing a fact
  - counters, denies, doubts, disagrees, disputes, opposes, quarrels with, rejects, responds
- describing and explaining a difficult concept
  - adds, contributes, expands, enhances, concludes, defines, depicts

CHAPTER 3
ORIENTING ARGUMENTS

MODULE III-1
RHETORICAL SITUATION DEFINED

A **rhetorical situation** is a context in which someone tries to persuade someone else or members of an audience. It consists of a writer or speaker, a message, an audience, and the limits or conditions that shape and give meaning to the moment in which the audience hears the message. Limits and conditions can be as varied as having only 500 words to describe an important issue, or the willingness of an audience to sit in the hot sun as they listen to your valedictorian speech. Practically speaking, writers and speakers use the idea of a rhetorical situation to make their ideas appealing and persuasive in the mind of their intended audience.

Therefore, before responding to or making any public statement or argument, you need to gather information about the situation.

The rhetorical situation (see Figure 3.1) consists of all the elements that affect how an audience understands an argument. The audience, writer/speaker, and message form a triangle at the heart of the rhetorical situation.

Figure 3.1
The rhetorical situation.

- **Audience**: the individual or group who will read, hear, or observe your argument. Your audience could be your professor, the readers of your blog, or a stadium full of people.
- **Writer/Speaker**: the one who creates and delivers the argument—in this case, you.
- **Message**: the language, imagery, sound, media, and technology that make up the argument intended to persuade the audience. A research paper, text message, and the State of the Union address all qualify as messages.

The rhetorical triangle always happens within a specific situation that is shaped by the immediate setting and surrounding culture.

- **Setting**: The setting is the time, place, and context in which your audience encounters your argument. Your audience might find your argument on the op-ed page of the local newspaper, for instance. The setting is also defined by the exigency that brings the writer or speaker and audience together. **Exigency** is the issue, urgent need, or recent event that motivates the speaker's message and so gives meaning to the setting. Your town's proposal to start charging a toll for crossing a nearby bridge might be the exigency that inspires your op-ed.
- **Culture**: All rhetorical situations exist within some larger cultural environment. Culture is composed of beliefs, values, and practices that make it possible for the individual to express ideas and experiences, and for an audience to understand these expressions. Your town may have its own culture, and different academic disciplines have very distinct cultures.

Every time you talk or write to someone, you are in a complex rhetorical situation.

If the rhetorical situation seems complicated, consider that you respond appropriately to complex rhetorical situations all the time without thinking about it.

Most of the information you need to examine and understand a rhetorical situation comes from you or your experience. The rest is easily discoverable.

MODULE III-2

AUDIENCE DEFINED

An **audience** is the individual or group who will read, hear, or observe your argument. If rhetoric is having the right word at the right time for the right audience, then everything depends upon addressing an audience you understand.

Intended and Secondary Audiences

Many people may hear or read your words and ideas; however, not everyone in your audience needs to hear you and not everyone is essential to your purpose. As you develop your argument, you will identify the **intended audience** you hope to persuade. These are the people who will help you achieve your purpose once persuaded. For example, if you intend to persuade your new boss of your skill and dedication, your new boss is your intended audience.

A **secondary audience** consists of others who read, hear, or observe your arguments. There are two kinds of secondary audience.

1. **Someone who can influence your intended audience**. If your intended audience is your boss, for instance, a secondary audience may be the boss's administrative assistant who also reads your document. If she hands it to your boss with positive comments, she could help persuade your intended audience.
2. **Your professor, who creates a fictional intended audience**. For example, a marketing professor may require your group to develop an advertising campaign for an imaginary company. You will write to persuade this imaginary company's CEO, but your professor, your secondary audience, will grade your work.

Simple and Complex Audiences

An audience can also be simple or complex. A **simple audience** is composed of one individual, or people with similar characteristics—such as age and education—and dispositions. **Disposition** is an individual's tendency of thought, preferred view, or initial understanding of an issue or your argument.

A **complex audience** may have a wide range of characteristics and dispositions and include individuals who will not be persuaded and those who already agree with you. In general, there are three kinds of audience members:

1. **The Doubters**: those who strongly disagree with you and are unlikely to change their minds despite your reasons and evidence.

2. **The Choir**: those who already agree with you and need no further persuasion.
3. **The Receptive**: those who have not considered your position, are undecided, or are leaning in a different direction but will give you a chance to make your argument.

The people most likely to be persuaded are the receptive. However, not everyone who can be persuaded can also help you achieve your goal. For example, you may convince your mother you would be an excellent class president, but if she cannot vote in the class election, she cannot help you get elected.

MODULE III-3

ANALYZING AN AUDIENCE

Persuasive writers and speakers analyze, define, and target those who can and need to be persuaded. When you do an **audience analysis** as you build an argument, you are trying to find answers to these questions:

- Who needs to be persuaded so you can achieve your goal?
- Among those who need to be persuaded, who *can* be persuaded?
- If they can be persuaded, what do they think and believe now?
- What do they expect and require of a writer or speaker?

There are a number of ways of discovering the characteristics and dispositions of audience members:

1. **Address your assigned audience**. If you have been assigned an audience, the characteristics and disposition of its members are close at hand. If your advertising agency has been hired to sell high-end headphones to 18- to 35-year-old musicians, vocalists, DJs, and producers, you need only examine this group. If you are writing for a professor, your audience was assigned when you picked the course, and her or his disposition will probably be on display during class.
2. **Invent your audience**. Imagine you are the first human to talk to an alien. You do not know the alien's language, culture, or purpose. All you can do is try to observe and then guess what actions and sounds will be meaningful. Students face a similar problem. Until they have observed and understand how professors talk, what they value, how they behave, and what they expect, students can only guess what a professor expects. Over time, if students are attentive and research their audience, wrong guesses are corrected and solid information begins to flesh out the nature of the audience. Direct and effective communication is then possible.

3. **Discover your audience**. If you have not been assigned an audience, your audience may become clear as you build your argument. For example, suppose you want to propose that Election Day each year should be a holiday. Initially, you may not have an audience in mind. However, as you research the subject, you may discover that your congressional representative is a member of the House Committee on Administration that can propose changes to federal election laws. Once you have discovered and defined your audience, you can target it with reasons and evidence.

Audience Analysis Checklist

Analyzing your audience is not like reading a Match.com profile. Just because someone shares your background, interests, and ethnicity does not mean the two of you will see an issue in a similar way. Each member of an audience is distinct, and an audience of distinct individuals does not share identical characteristics and dispositions.

However, if you are writing or speaking to more than one person, it is difficult to shape your argument without making some generalizations about your audience and the setting. The more informed your generalizations, the more persuasive your argument will be. The checklist in Figure 3.2 will help you analyze your intended audience so you can clarify your purpose and shape your argument. If you can answer all the checklist questions, you will have a good profile of your audience. Your argument will be more effective if it is based on a real audience as opposed to an invented one.

Figure 3.2
This checklist will help you begin to clarify your audience with some basic generalizations.

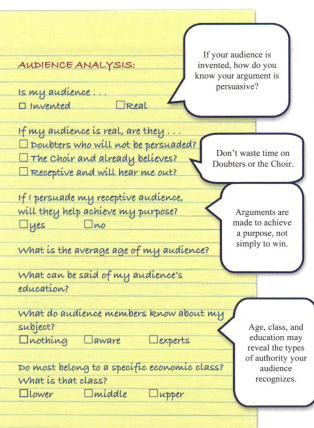

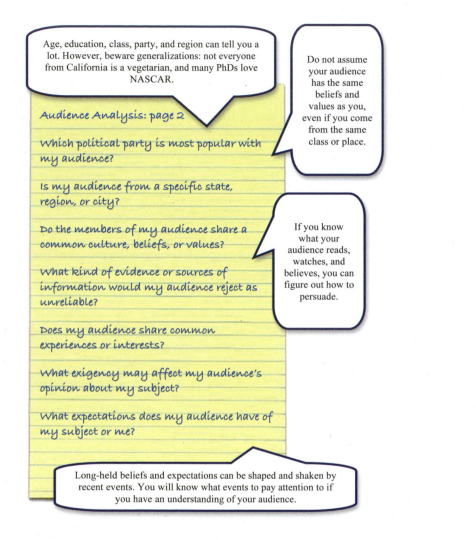

Age, education, class, party, and region can tell you a lot. However, beware generalizations: not everyone from California is a vegetarian, and many PhDs love NASCAR.

Do not assume your audience has the same beliefs and values as you, even if you come from the same class or place.

Audience Analysis: page 2

Which political party is most popular with my audience?

Is my audience from a specific state, region, or city?

Do the members of my audience share a common culture, beliefs, or values?

If you know what your audience reads, watches, and believes, you can figure out how to persuade.

What kind of evidence or sources of information would my audience reject as unreliable?

Does my audience share common experiences or interests?

What exigency may affect my audience's opinion about my subject?

What expectations does my audience have of my subject or me?

Long-held beliefs and expectations can be shaped and shaken by recent events. You will know what events to pay attention to if you have an understanding of your audience.

Targeting Your Audience: Mistakes to Avoid

Many arguments fail to persuade because the speaker or writer has misunderstood or oversimplified the intended audience. Avoid these common mistakes when thinking about your audience.

1. "I am writing to everybody."
   If you really want to talk to everyone, you would need to translate your argument into an estimated 7,000 world languages. Writing to a general audience is like trying to send a meaningful email to everyone, everywhere.

2. "I am talking to those who have had similar experiences."
Why? Sharing experiences is wonderful, but if your audience already agrees with you, what are you going to achieve?

3. "My audience is made up of people who can relate to me."
Students who choose their own audience and purpose often prefer to talk to people of their own age, background, values, and dispositions. Such conversations are important and comfortable, but if audience members share your dispositions and values, it is unlikely that you will have strong differences of opinion where you can demonstrate your rhetorical skills.

4. "They know what I mean."
Your readers or listeners do not know what you mean. A receptive audience will recognize your topic, but they do not know why you believe what you believe, why you think your proposal is the best move, or why the evidence you have found is so important to you.

> Experiences and interests are often linked to values and dispositions

5. "They don't like me or care what I say."
Disagreement is not hostility. A person who thinks differently from you may simply have no evidence or reason to think, believe, or act as you do. If you think your readers or listeners are hostile, you are unlikely to explore why they think as they do, or to shape your message to provide the evidence and reasons they need to change their mind.

6. "I think this joke is funny, so my audience will too."
Comedy is hard. A joke can break the ice or develop a point, but think of your audience's needs. In many formal settings like a university or a business, a joke may undercut the authority and trust you are trying to establish.

7. "If they just read to the end, it will all make sense."
Most of us will read only the first paragraph of an article or story if it is not interesting. Your professors will read every page, but at what point will he or she make a decision about your grade? Each sentence, point, and paragraph should contribute to your persuasive power. If, on the other hand, a professor loses track of an argument somewhere in the middle, how likely is it that the remaining pages will be so impressive that she forgets the confusing part?

Effective writers and speakers target receptive members of an audience. You probably do not know them, they may come from very different backgrounds, and their way of thinking may be confounding to you. Still, you can persuade your audience if you work to understand their characteristics and dispositions as well as the setting and culture that shape meaning and understanding. The Breaking the Block feature entitled "Inventing the Audience" will help you refine your understanding of your intended audience.

Breaking the Block
Inventing the Audience

Moving from an invented audience to a real, intended audience is an important process of writing and revision.

This exercise can help you discover a subject that is of interest to a specific audience, or help you develop educated guesses that will lead to a richer understanding of your audience. It combines observing and note-taking with analysis and writing. For this exercise, observe or think for 10 minutes and write for 10 minutes.

Step One: Analyze a small group
Think of a small group of 4 to 15 people. It could be the people at a lunch table, the foursome on the golf course in front of you, the small group talking in the back of a bus, or a choir you heard recently.
- Observe or try to recall some qualities of the group members, such as their dress, mood, tone, and habits.
- List three subjects in the news or of current interest that they are probably aware of.
- List three events that have likely caused most of them distress.
- List three causes or charities a majority of them could probably support.
- Now think of a single topic that could cause a huge argument among the members of this group.

Step Two: Reflect
What was the most difficult part of inventing this audience, and what was easy? If you had to address this group on the single topic that would cause an argument, how would you begin and what kind of language would you use?

MODULE III-4

USING APPEALS, MEDIA, AND CONVENTIONS TO INFLUENCE YOUR AUDIENCE

An analysis and understanding of your audience prepares you to shape the meaning of your argument by using appeals, media, and conventions that will help persuade them.

Appeals

Tradition provides three types of appeals to the audience's disposition and values and also provides a way of determining the best time to use each appeal. You make an **appeal** whenever you structure an idea or select specific types of information so that both are attractive and persuasive to a specific audience. There are many ways of appealing to someone. If you use a chocolate cake to express your affection to a friend, you are appealing to his or her sweet tooth. In Western cultures, three types of appeal have become cultural practices: *pathos*, *ethos*, and *logos*.

- *Pathos* is the way in which an author or speaker arouses or uses emotions to move the audience to believe the source, be persuaded by the message, and think or act as the message argues. At the end of an editorial, when the writer ends with a call for action based on pride, a sense of duty, or sympathy, for example, they are using emotions to motivate the readers to act. *Pathos* can use any emotion, including anger, delight, or outrage, as well as empathy. However, only audiences that share, or have been persuaded to share, your view, disposition, or argument are likely to be moved by *pathos*. Academic audiences, those expecting evidence-based arguments, and the highly skeptical are unlikely to be moved by *pathos* and may see such an appeal as manipulation.
- *Ethos* is the way in which an author or speaker moves the audience to believe that the source of the message is trustworthy and authoritative. A student who describes in detail an expert's credentials and uses proper documentation is making an *ethos* appeal. Think of *ethos* as a way for the audience to evaluate the honesty, accuracy, and passion the speaker has for her or his subject. It is difficult to imagine an audience that does not acknowledge some type of authority, whether it be based on faith, experience, or expertise. However, not every audience will be persuaded by every type of *ethos* appeal. If the basis of your or your sources' authority meets your audience's expectations and you deal with your subject seriously and opposing opinions fairly, then you will appear credible.
- *Logos* is the way in which an author or speaker moves the audience to believe that the message is true, valid, and beyond doubt. When someone says your

argument is well reasoned and logical, that person has been moved by a *logos* appeal. Because *logos* appeals are based upon solid reasoning and evidence, they are often more complex arguments than those heard in casual conversation. For example, if you are delivering a toast at your office holiday party, a *logos* appeal will fall flat. However, if you are making a presentation that may change the direction and business model of the entire office, facts, figures, data, and logical reasoning will be expected and necessary for persuasion.

Appeals shape meaning, but audiences will also consider the timing or appropriateness when evaluating your appeals.

Kairos

Kairos is an ancient Greek word that does not have an exact translation in English. However, if you have ever been sad and had someone say just the right thing at just the right time to turn your mood around, you have experienced *kairos*. A *kairotic* moment has been lost if, after a conflict or an argument, you think of the perfect comeback—but it is too late.

Kairos was used by the Greeks to describe moments that seem to call for a certain kind of response, speech, or argument. In short, *kairos* can be translated as the right time or opportunity, which is why *kairos* is often linked to appeals. For example, Dilios's speech prior to the final battle with Xerxes' Persian army is a *pathos* appeal to the 300 Spartans' courage, sense of duty, honor, love of country, and loyalty to their king.

Had Dilios instead used a *logos* appeal by analyzing the strengths and weaknesses of the 150,000 Persian soldiers, his speech would not have been timely and would not have spurred the 300 to fight bravely to the last. In other words, it would not have taken advantage of the *kairotic* moment.

The *kairos* of an academic setting is shaped by the assignments, due dates, professor's expectations, and subject of a course as well as more personal exigencies such as your desire to succeed and the pressure you feel to do well. In an upper-level sociology course on race relations and public policy, the exigencies that bring you and other students to the class are graduation requirements, an interest in the subject, and an interest in readings concerning race relations in the United States. However, if an unarmed person of color were shot and killed during a traffic stop near your campus, the exigencies would change the *kairotic* moment of the next class, as many students would look to the course and professor for a way to understand and respond to the tragedy.

If you keep *kairos* in mind, you will realize that issues, events, and the audience's needs are always changing within the rhetorical situation, and they in turn change how individuals think, making them receptive to different types of appeals and arguments. Knowing about exigency enables you to explore what is most on the mind of your audience—like a happy occasion or recent tragedy—and use this knowledge to build your argument.

The Message in the Medium

A **medium** is what you use to extend your thoughts to others, such as a printed page, a PowerPoint presentation, or a web page. The medium sits between you and the audience. "The medium is the message" is a famous phrase, but it is often misunderstood. What the twentieth-century communication philosopher Marshall McLuhan meant by it is that each medium can create subtle but long-term social effects that we may not notice but that shape the meanings we derive from the messages we receive. For example, in the 1950s, television created a new kind of home entertainment that discouraged family conversation. A message of the medium of TV can thus be that family time is quiet time.

Figure 3.3
TV brought the family together—quietly.

Practically speaking, every medium and even every form or genre has social effects that condition how your audience will understand what you write or say before you begin. For instance, older people are more likely to trust what they see on the Internet if web pages resemble traditional sources of trusted information like magazines and newspapers.

In an academic setting, consider the difference between a traditional research paper printed on paper and a Prezi presentation. The medium of paper forces the argument to unfold in a linear, point-by-point, way. A Prezi, on the other hand, allows the presenter to bounce between any number of points without concern for an order or hierarchy. Media are patterns you can play with, but keep in mind that every medium—paper or Prezi, for example—will communicate different meanings to an audience.

Conventions

Conventions are expected or required ways of doing things, from the width of the margins to punctuation to documentation format. The proper use of conventions communicates your care for your audience and your subject. For example, if you see a misspelling in a newspaper article, you may begin to doubt the reporter's skills and the newspaper's professionalism.

Audience Expectations

When someone buys a ticket for Disney on Ice or mitski, they arrive at the venue with specific expectations. If mitski does not play "Nobody" or Elsa does not glide around an ice-crystal palace while singing "Let It Go," there will be some very angry audience members. However, if mitski ends the final set with a rendition of "Let It Go," her fans may find a new reason to love her. Audience expectations are an opportunity, not a limitation. However, you cannot fulfill, confound, or play with an audience's expectations unless you know them, and know them well.

Your professor may expect a research paper, but she may be delighted with a research paper cast as a brief documentary film shot with an iPhone. Then again, your chemical biology professor's detailed written description of what a lab report should look like accompanied by perfect examples written by previous students should be an indication that her expectations are not to be played with. If you know what you must do, what you can do, and what freedoms you have—in other words, the expectations of your audience—you have all you need to build a persuasive argument that achieves your purpose.

Gaps in Your Audience's Understanding

You must assume your audience knows something about your subject; otherwise, they would be unlikely to read or hear you. However, what we do not know also shapes how we understand others. I think I know how my car works, but when my mechanic said my serpentine needed tightening, I wondered if there might be a snake under the hood, while she assumed I knew she meant the serpentine belt.

Unanticipated gaps in your audience's understanding can lead to confusion. However, gaps also provide the writer or speaker with an opportunity to educate, as well as to demonstrate a deep understanding of the subject.

CHAPTER 4
FRAMING ARGUMENTS

MODULE IV-1

FRAMING YOUR SUBJECT

When you **frame** your subject, you identify what you need to research and write about and what you do not need to deal with. Having a carefully defined frame has three benefits:

1. It will help you stay focused and prevent you from wasting time and energy.
2. It will keep you on track as you research and draft and will provide a path for your argument.
3. It helps you manage audience expectations.

You might think of framing your argument in terms of an actual frame you place around a collage of words and images. For example, it is hard to imagine a frame that could contain all the important events, locations, and names of the 2016 US presidential campaign. Even if you could frame such a massive collection of events and subjects, the many different elements within the frame would be so overwhelming that it would seem nonsensical. Even a specific subject like the media coverage of campaign rallies offers so many good subjects to explore that it would seem impossible to decide on any one. Yet your professor expects you to pick a subject and get to work (see Figure 4.1).

COURSE: POLS 470 – "Contemporary
Presidential Campaigns"
ASSIGNMENT: Primary Document Analysis
        (10 points of 200 total class points)
DUE: During class one week from today
LENGTH: 1-2 pages

Review the 2016 campaign documents, press
releases, and articles assigned for today's class.
Select one document and analyze it and be
prepared to discuss your findings during class
next week.

Figure 4.1
An assignment
for a political
science course
that needs
framing.

Assignments like the one in Figure 4.1 may seem overwhelming. However, you can tame tasks like this one by building a frame that helps you find your subject. For example, the word cloud and yellow frame in Figure 4.2 shows how a frame can provide a coherent scope and a clear focus on the topic of the 2016 presidential campaign by defining a set of related events, ideas, and names that you could reasonably research and write about.

Figure 4.2   A great deal happened during the run-up to the 2016 Republican and Democratic Party conventions. A frame can define a context that allows you to focus on a subject. Moving the yellow frame shifts your focus and may allow a topic to come to light.

Frame = Scope + Focus

In a paper or a speech, **scope** is the context or breadth of knowledge that you draw upon to make your argument. Academic disciplines provide the initial scope for much of the work you will do in college. The scope in Figure 4.2 limits the context of all possible subjects to the events, ideas, and names within the yellow frame. Writers or speakers **focus** when they concentrate on a single data point, detail, subject, or image. The focus of an argument will help you develop the position you want your reader or listener to accept and adopt. Within the scope in Figure 4.2, for example, you could focus on the concept of disruption as it relates to candidate Bernie Sanders's pursuit of convention delegates.

Controlling scope and focus helps you manage your audience's expectations. If you indicate your scope and focus early in your argument and stick to both, you will have created an expectation in your reader's mind that you subsequently satisfy. To begin, think about what has been assigned and what is expected, which will guide what you promise your audience.

The scope of your research may already be set by the professor's assignment. Your focus will grow sharper as you research, read, and draft your ideas.

Example: If the professor of your course on "The 19th Century Immigrant Experience" asks you to write an argument, the context of the class provides the initial frame.

> **Immigration** to
> **the United States** during the
> **19th century** considered from the
> **discipline of history**.

As you research the topic of immigration in the nineteenth century, your *scope* narrows to:

> **Immigrant labor** recruited from
> **China to the United States** between the years
> **1840 and 1890**.

Further research may allow you to refine your *focus* to:

- **Chinese immigrants** pursuing the 1850s gold rush **compared** to **Chinese immigrants** recruited during the 1860s to work on the Central Pacific Railroad.

To frame your subject in an academic context, begin by identifying your needs. Once you understand or have established the frame you need to work within, you can more confidently fill that frame with your creativity and insights.

Understanding the Assignment

If your assignment is not clear, you still need information about these requirements, so to frame your subject, you will need to visit your professor or whoever set you the task. Whether you are asking for clarity or trying to understand the assignment given, you'll want to come away with the following:

- **The assigned subject of the project**. What is the specific focus of the assignment and what is the scope, or range or context, you are expected to draw upon as you do your invention and research? The POLS 470 assignment (Figure 4.1), for example, asks you to focus on a single campaign document from class, and the scope is limited to the 2016 presidential campaign.
- **The forms of thinking you must demonstrate**. For an assignment in a film studies class, for instance, are you expected to review a movie or analyze the camera positions in a movie? (Chapter 5 describes forms of thinking common to different academic disciplines.)
- **The knowledge, competencies, or skills you must apply**. Does your communications professor expect you to write a research paper or create a multimedia, oral presentation? In the POLS 470 assignment (Figure 4.1), you are expected to review or read carefully a specific campaign document and analyze it using the methods and approaches discussed in class.
- **The freedoms and limitations of the assignment**. For example, in the the POLS 470 assignment (Figure 4.1), can you talk about the 2020 presidential election? Can you use the first person *I* in your paper? Can you use a document or reading you found outside of class? What are the limits and requirements, such as page length or specific databases and documentation styles you should use?

When you start to work on an assignment, your scope will often be very broad. If you don't have a specific subject in mind, your focus could be as large as your scope. However, as you develop your ideas and refine your subject, your scope will get smaller, allowing you to focus on a very specific subject. In other words, your frame will become clearer as you move through the writing process.

Knowing Audience Expectations

Research audience expectations, both the obvious and the unstated. If you do not have a specific assignment, you must still deal with audience expectations as you decide on your frame. Even if you have written instructions or a prompt, some expectations may be implied. Try to identify the following:

- **Who will read and evaluate your work?** For example, if you are free to choose your subject in a first-year writing course, will your professor be your primary audience, or are you allowed to choose a target audience for your paper? (Module III-3 gives you the tools to analyze your audience.)

- **The discipline or specialization that should inform your perspective.** When researching, do you have to stay within a specific discipline or does your audience, perhaps your professor, value interdisciplinary approaches (drawing from more than one academic discipline)?

Identify Your Promises

If you told your professor or boss you would do an analysis of the fourth-quarter earnings of the top three competitors of the Mattel toy company, you have created an expectation you must meet in some way. Handing in an analysis of only one competitor will not satisfy that expectation. Other promises include the following:

- If you made a proposal, what did you say you would write about? If you are responding to a call or request for information, what does the request imply about your focus and scope?
- If you have already drafted a research proposal, plan, or bibliography, you have already indicated your scope. Will your professor be alarmed or impressed if you expand your scope to include experts and research from other disciplines or sources from other time periods?
- If you have been discussing your research, thesis, and drafts with your professor during individual meetings, how will he or she respond if you hand in a final essay that has a different focus?

Once you know what has been assigned, what is expected, and what you may have promised, you are ready to draft a research question.

Drafting a Research Question

When you have defined a scope and focus for your argument, you are ready to use your framed subject to write a research question. A good research question helps you and your audience in three main ways:

1. It guides your research and reasoning by giving you a focused question to answer.
2. It helps you evaluate the relevance of your sources, ideas, and evidence.
3. It invites your audience into your search for an answer, so they can more readily accept the answer or argument you propose.

Working backwards from the final argument to the question that started the research, we can see the benefits of a good research question. Great documentaries often begin with a research question. Ken Burn's *The Dust Bowl* is driven by a single question:

What was the social and economic impact of the Dust Bowl that took place during the 1930s? To answer his question, Burns interviewed people who lived through the "Dirty Thirties" and consulted experts who have studied the Dust Bowl's impact. He also researched relevant artifacts and letters. Because he poses his question early in the documentary, the audience's curiosity is aroused, and they adopt the question as their own.

The best time to write a research question is after you have done some initial invention and research. Considering your own thinking on a subject, listening to your peers' opinions, and reviewing the thoughts of scholars and experts will give you access to many conversations around your subject. Your research will reveal the questions that provoked other scholars to search for answers and the questions that still remain to be answered.

Discovering Unanswered Questions

Most assignments contain the makings of a research question. If the assignment is not already in the form of a question, try to convert it into one, using the frame of the assignment.

Look to Research

Academic articles often end with a call for additional research. Although an article usually presents the scholar's or researcher's answer to a research question, often the author will pose more questions that need to be addressed. You may find a compelling research question from that source. (See also Chapter 2 for more on this kind of invention.)

Discussion sites and bulletin boards are other places where you can discover the debates and pressing questions of most interest to groups, specialties, and academic disciplines. Ask your professor for suggestions, or use a discussion board search engine such as Boardreader or Omgili, to find online conversations about your topic. Pay attention to the debates and questions that consistently pop up.

Look to Peers

If you use the five invention questions in Figure 4.3 to discover and develop a subject, you are well on your way to a research question. Use these general questions as a starting point, and then make them more specific based upon your answers. Note that some questions will be more appropriate for certain disciplines than others.

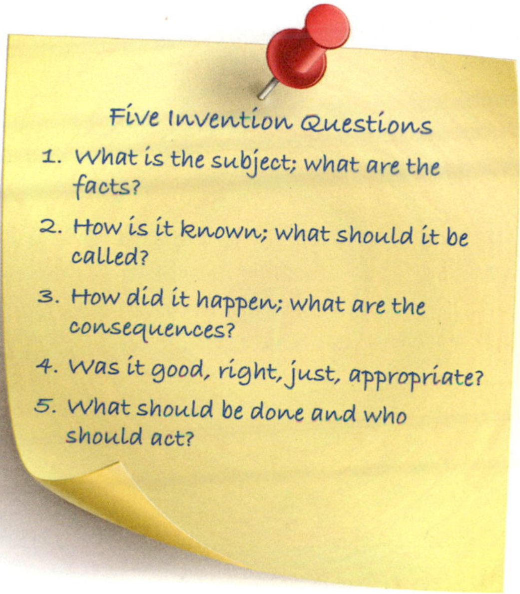

Five Invention Questions

1. What is the subject; what are the facts?

2. How is it known; what should it be called?

3. How did it happen; what are the consequences?

4. Was it good, right, just, appropriate?

5. What should be done and who should act?

Figure 4.3
These stasis questions have been used for more than 2,000 years to invent ideas, develop authority about subjects, and shape arguments for an audience.

Now share your scope and focus and your answers to the questions in Figure 4.3 with one or more peers, such as a classmate or roommate. Ask your peers,

- what caught their attention,
- what surprised them,
- what they disagree with, and
- what they would like to hear more about.

You may develop a great question from just one of the five invention questions, or your roommate may suggest focusing on answers to two or more. As always, when you are researching a subject or answering a question you really care about, your work and writing will be easier and more engaging.

Finally, write a question that you want to answer. The following checklist will help you formulate a strong research question.

Research Question Checklist

Is my research question...

- **worth answering?** Does it contribute something new or help me demonstrate my skills and understanding?
- **relevant to my audience?** Will my audience want an answer to this question?
- **relevant to the subject?** Does the question define my scope, and is it focused on my intended subject?

- **already answered?** If so, can I add to the existing answer, offer a different answer, or come at the question from a different perspective or with different evidence?
- **overly complicated?** Will my question require more time and energy than is available? Am I going beyond the assignment?

As you draft your ideas and continue your research, you may need to revise your research question. Do not be alarmed! This indicates that you are discovering significant data, information, or documents and that your depth of understanding is growing. Remember, the writing process is recursive and you need to be flexible in your approach.

MODULE IV-2

PRIMARY AND SECONDARY STASIS QUESTIONS

When you are confronted with a complex or confounding assignment and a deadline, you have a lot in common with investigators trying to make sense of a confusing crime scene or lawyers trying to persuade a jury. Knowing how to get at the heart of a problem or issue, what to do with the answers you discover, and how to shape a persuasive argument is often a matter of asking the right question at the right time.

The word *stasis* literally means stability or balance, and rhetorical stasis is achieved when two people, or a person and an audience, come to an agreement or a common understanding. Stasis questions will not make your audience agree with you, but the questions will help you discover the source of a disagreement and then suggest a form of argument that is most likely to persuade your audience to accept your view.

If you have ever been in a quarrel with someone and at some point asked, "What are you talking about?," you have experienced a desire for stasis. For example, imagine your brother has been angry with you all week. You don't know what his problem is or what to say to him.

What Happened: After your brother left for school, you borrowed his sweater and accidently snagged it. Now he is angry.

What the Parties Are Thinking:

> You: I apologized and bought him a new sweater, but he is still angry for no good reason. After all, he never really wore that sweater.

Your brother: She seems to think my stuff is her stuff, and this isn't the first time she took something without asking.

Why You Don't Have Stasis: That an unloved sweater got torn is not in dispute. In fact, the sweater is not the source of the quarrel. This disagreement is about definitions. Your definition of borrowing and your brother's definition of stealing, or taking without permission, are the central issue.

Over time, brother and sister may find their way to stasis if they both come to understand the real source of the dispute. If they used stasis questions, though, they could reach that understanding more quickly.

Stasis questions are a sequence of questions used to examine complex problems or issues. Greek and Roman rhetoric made use of four primary stasis questions. Today, the five primary stasis questions include a question of value:

1. Questions of fact: What happened? What are the facts?
2. Questions of definition: How is it known? What should it be called?
3. Questions of cause and consequence: How did it happen? What is the consequence?
4. Questions of value: Was it good, right, just, appropriate?
5. Questions of procedure and proposal: What is the best response? Who should act?

Stasis questions are not just some dusty old tool. As we saw in the sweater example, when used in sequence, stasis questions can indicate the type of disagreement and the form of argument best suited to persuading those on the other side of the dispute. In addition to determining the most persuasive form of an argument, these questions help you do a number of important writing tasks:

- **Invent and Understand**—Stasis questions help you invent (discover, research, retrieve, and synthesize information) by clarifying and developing your understanding of complex issues and events.

    For example, if you were asked to write a position paper on a student government resolution requiring trigger warnings, stasis questions can guide your research by breaking down the issue into its most basic elements, such as what is meant by a trigger, before considering more complex issues such as the values or criteria that should be used to evaluate any potential harm that a professor's lecture or discussion could cause.

- **Know Your Audience**—Stasis questions can help you investigate the disposition of your reader or listener, revealing what is unseen or unstated. Without an understanding of the points of agreement and disagreement between you and your audience, persuasion is not possible.

For example, until you know how your audience understands and defines psychological trauma (embarrassment, social discomfort, or a full blown PTSD flashback), you don't really know if you should write a definition paper, a cause-and-effect paper, or a proposal.

- **Build Authority**—Stasis questions can reveal parts of your argument that need further development, additional research, and more supporting evidence. Stasis questions also direct you to the common form (purpose and strategy) that best suits your argument and audience.

Above all, stasis questions are a method of invention. More than simple brainstorming, however, they help you think deeply and systematically about issues and audiences. The Breaking the Block exercise entitled "Think like a Journalist" will help you see the practical value of stasis questions. Stasis questions are organized into primary and secondary questions. Secondary questions probe the same territory as, but at a deeper level than, primary questions.

Defining Primary Stasis Questions

The primary stasis questions are not simply a list but a sequence. The answer to the first makes it possible to find an answer to the second, and so on. So they must be asked in order. The sequence of questions is important because once your questions have identified the areas of agreement, you are left with the question of where the two sides have very different answers. At that point, the real investigation begins.

Returning to the sweater example, brother and sister agree on the facts, but each uses different words and different definitions to describe the event. The question is why: How does each perspective lead to a different definition, and what must happen to move one person to accept the other's definition?

In an academic setting, imagine you have been assigned an analysis of the immigration debate during the 2020 election. You discover that for the most part the parties agree on the facts; for instance, the parties agree on the number of legal and illegal immigrants. They also agree on what the terms *legal* and *illegal* or *undocumented* mean. However, they strongly disagree on the cause and consequences of the current immigration policy. The causal question, then, is the point where secondary questions can focus and guide your research.

Defining Secondary Stasis Questions

Each primary stasis question leads to five secondary questions. Answering secondary stasis questions allows you to make a more focused examination once you discover where you and your audience disagree. For example, once brother or sister zero in on definition as their most pressing point of disagreement, secondary questions can help clarify what definitions are in dispute and how they are defining the same points differently.

You will note that many of the secondary stasis questions in the list below are similar to the primary questions. Whether the disagreement is about facts or values, the same sequence of questions can be used to examine the type and the precise source of a dispute.

1. **Facts**: What happened? What are the facts?
   a. Did something happen, or is there an issue?
   b. What are the facts of the event or issue?
   c. Is there a problem concerning the event, issue, or facts?
   d. What cause or change brought about the event or issue?
   e. Can what happened be reversed, changed, or affected?
2. **Definition**: How is it known? What should it be called?
   a. How is the event or issue characterized? Is it a problem, a debate, tension, an impasse, a misunderstanding?
   b. What exactly is the event or issue in question?
   c. Does the event or issue belong to a larger class or category?
   d. Can the event or issue in question be broken into smaller parts?
   e. How is the event or issue related to the larger class or its smaller parts?
3. **Cause/Consequence**: How did it happen? What is the consequence?
   a. Why did it happen?
   b. What might explain what happened?
   c. What possible causes do not make sense or can be eliminated?
   d. What was the immediate or most obvious effect?
   e. Will other consequences become apparent later or in other locations or situations?
4. **Value**: Was it good, right, just, appropriate?
   a. Is the event, issue, or consequence beneficial or detrimental?
   b. How serious is it?
   c. Who has been or will be affected?
   d. If nothing is done, what will happen?
   e. What will it take to change what has happened?
5. **Procedure/Proposal**: What is the best response? Who should act?
   a. Is a response necessary?
   b. Who should respond?
   c. What kind of response is possible?
   d. What kind of response is necessary?
   e. What must be done to respond?

Breaking the Block
Think like a Journalist

Journalists do not have time for writer's block, which is why they use the *who, what, when, where, why,* and *how* questions to quickly gather information. These six questions and the five stasis questions share the same historical source: the invention and analysis of information. This exercise will take only 20 minutes and help you see how often this sequence of questions appears in daily life.

Step One: Look Around
If you have been assigned a subject, skip to step two. If you are free to choose your own subject, watch the news or look through news websites, magazines, and newspapers and read about an ongoing event, issue, or argument. How to prevent violent attacks in schools, how to house the homeless, or how to stop climate change are just three possible issues to explore.

Step Two: Think like a Journalist
Find the heart of the matter. If, for example, you are required to write a sociological analysis of a specific image or ad, the assignment instructions can help. Or you might think about how your professor has demonstrated such an analysis, or ask your professor what one element of the image would lend itself to analysis. In the case of an image or ad, how would advertisers perceive the image and how would consumer activists?

Think about how different groups with different concerns and perspectives on the event, issue, or argument would answer the questions. If possible, interview such people or try to determine how each interested group might answer each question. Make a list of answers representing how each group would answer the primary questions.

Step Three: Dig Deeper with Secondary Questions
Where the groups have similar answers, these answers are the foundation of your argument: the common ground you build on. Where the two groups have very different answers to a primary question, dig deeper. Make a second list of answers to the relevant secondary questions. If you don't know how someone would answer, read a bit more or ask friends or classmates who hold such a perspective.

Step Four: Reflect
Look at your answers. If you were to pick a side or a perspective, how would you persuade those on the other side to change their minds? What points or ideas stand in the way of agreement? Is there a third way, or could the groups meet in the middle?

MODULE IV-3

BUILDING AN ARGUMENT USING STASIS QUESTIONS

When you are building an argument, stasis questions can help you invent, develop arguments suited to your audience, and establish authority on complex issues. Let's begin by looking at how the primary and secondary questions can shape your argument. The five questions are linked to common forms of argument, as shown in Figure 4.4.

STASIS QUESTIONS →	COMMON FORMS
What are the facts?	State the Facts
How is it known?	Define
How did it happen?	Determine Cause
Was it right?	Analyze and Evaluate
What response is best?	Propose a Solution

Figure 4.4 Arguments are commonly built upon a hierarchy. You must agree on facts if your argument is about definitions. If you are arguing over the best solution, you already agree that there is a problem. The question in dispute points to the appropriate form.

Inventing with Questions

In her "Advanced Composition" class, Jamie Battaglia was assigned a position paper on any contemporary issue. The subject of medical marijuana caught her attention when her university announced that it would not recognize prescriptions for medical marijuana. Using stasis questions to guide her research, she found answers that helped her develop a deeper understanding of the issue.

Research Notes: Medical Marijuana

1. **Facts**: What are the facts of medical marijuana?
   - The phrase medical marijuana seems to have been coined in the 1990s to distinguish medical from recreational marijuana use.
   - In politics and in the medical community, medical marijuana is very controversial.
   - Recreational marijuana has been legalized in 18 states. Federal law does not recognize the medical nor recreational use of marijuana.

2. **Definition**: How is medical marijuana known?
   - Marijuana or cannabis is a plant. Some farmers consider it a weed. Others grow it for its hemp fiber or for medical use.

- The federal government, directed by the Controlled Substances Act, defines marijuana as a controlled substance similar to cocaine and heroin.
- Some see marijuana as a type of medication that can relieve serious symptoms and treat sickness. Others compare its recreational use to alcohol.

3. **Cause/Consequence**: How did medical marijuana come to be? What is the consequence?
   - After years of debate, some states legalized the medical and recreational use of marijuana.
   - States where the use of medical marijuana is legal have seen an explosion in the number of marijuana dispensaries.
   - The demand for medical marijuana has resulted in more sophisticated farming and crossbreeding methods. Some types of marijuana are much more potent than the marijuana of a few years ago.

4. **Value**: Was it good, right, just, appropriate?
   - Those who oppose legal marijuana say there are no real medical benefits and that marijuana is a gateway drug that leads to serious addiction.
   - Supporters argue that there is medical and anecdotal evidence proving medical marijuana relieves symptoms, cures diseases, and is safe.
   - The pharmaceutical industry claims any medical benefits from marijuana can more safely be found in USDA approved and regulated medications.

5. **Procedure/Proposal**: What is the best response to legalized marijuana and who should act?
   - The federal government and Drug Enforcement Administration promise to enforce all federal laws, close marijuana dispensaries, and arrest drug dealers and users.
   - Supporters argue that citizens should pressure state and federal lawmakers to legalize recreational and medical marijuana and pressure the medical community for more research about its benefits.
   - Some libertarians argue that the government should not regulate any personal freedoms including the use of any drugs for any purpose.

Looking More Closely with Secondary Questions

Looking over the answers to the primary questions, Jamie was surprised to see that nearly all of her sources agreed on the facts of the issue.

However, when it came to how marijuana is defined, she quickly saw that different groups use very different names for the products, and their effects, that come from the marijuana plant. Clearly, the different names (marijuana, medical htc, or hemp) were linked to different definitions.

Once Jamie recognized that the source of the dispute was the conflicting definitions, she moved to the secondary questions of definition.

Secondary Questions: Definition

a. How is the issue of medical marijuana characterized?
As a public health issue, as the difference between medication and drug abuse, as a problem for medical research, as a question of personal rights and freedoms, and as a legislative issue.

b. What exactly is the issue in question?
The issue seems to be the different names people use when talking about marijuana.

c. Does the issue belong to a larger class or category?
It seems like a problem of language, meaning, and legal classification.

d. Can the issue in question be broken into smaller parts?
Different groups who use different words and definitions and their motivation for doing so.

e. How is the issue related to the larger class or its smaller parts?
In terms of language and meaning, the relationship is between culture and law. In terms of smaller parts, the issue is personal motivations and values.

The primary questions helped Jamie identify the type of disagreement at hand. The secondary questions of definition helped her see that the source of the conflict could be found in the cultures that informed the words and definitions used by federal government officials, DEA agents, and state legislators. She could then examine her university's position and the words and definitions used, as opposed to the way in which some students described their use of marijuana.

At this stage, stasis questions helped Jamie understand the issue and helped her make sense of the sources she discovered. In addition, she understands the source of the conflict and the dispositions of potential audiences, such as students with prescriptions or administrators at her university. She can now begin to develop her own position within the ongoing debates.

Questioning Your Audience

In addition to inventing, developing, and clarifying, finding stasis is about finding the common ground you share with your audience. **Common ground** refers to the points that are not in dispute. Common ground is in fact what makes disagreement and persuasion possible. If two parties did not share some common ground, agreeing on some points, they would be talking about completely different things.

Over dinner with her mother, Jamie talked about her research. She described the five questions and the different positions her research revealed. Jamie knew that she and her mother share a great deal of common ground. They agree on the facts, definitions, and consequences of marijuana used as a medication.

When it came to questions of value, ethics, and morals, Jamie was surprised to find that her mother went a different way. Her mother thought marijuana was like alcohol—potentially dangerous, but a matter of personal choice. Jamie, on the other hand, saw marijuana as a powerful medicine, like Percocet or codeine, that must be controlled by the government for the good of society.

If you think of the sequence of stasis questions as a map, it is easier to visualize how two people, like Jamie and her mother, can share some common ground and diverge in other areas (see Figure 4.5).

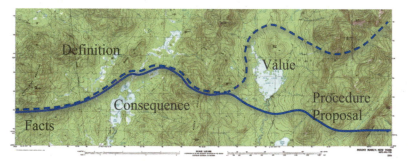

Figure 4.5 In this example, the solid blue path tracks Jamie's answers and the dotted blue represents her mother's answers to the stasis questions.

If Jamie wants to persuade her mother to accept her line of thought, it would be pointless to write a definition argument, as they already agree on definitions. She would need to write an argument focusing on value. If Jamie succeeds and persuades her mother to agree with her view of marijuana as a powerful medicine, the issue of value becomes common ground. Until they agree on values, they will not agree on proposals for controlling marijuana.

Whether you are taking notes, interviewing your audience, or answering the stasis questions for yourself, stay within the scope of the question. For example, when asked about facts, do not define. When considering definition questions, don't answer with opinions about value.

Building Authority: Research and Form

Because different people will answer the stasis questions differently, different audiences will be moved or persuaded by different evidence and different forms. For example, Jamie and her father may agree on the facts but diverge when it comes to consequences. Because he answers the questions differently and they diverge from common ground at a different point than she and her mother do, Jamie would need to research different evidence and use a different form—narration and determination of cause—for her father. Her father may think that a consequence of legalized marijuana is simply increased sales of much more potent marijuana to people who want to get high. However, a narrative that describes a cancer patient who is able to manage nausea and go back to work thanks to professionally grown marijuana may persuade Jamie's father.

In an academic context, things are a bit more complex. For a professor, the goal of an assignment may be to develop a student's research, critical thinking, and writing skills and then to evaluate the resulting argument. The professor's personal views may be irrelevant. Stasis questions, then, may be most useful as an invention tool: a way of exploring the disputed points and terms within an issue assigned by the professor or discovered by the student. For more on writing in academic contexts and understanding academic audiences, see Module I-3.

Whether you are building an argument to persuade a specific audience with distinct views or demonstrating your understanding of an issue and the points in dispute, answering the stasis questions will lend your argument authority because you will know the ins and outs of an issue, know what is settled or common ground, and know how to shape and form your thesis, reasons, and evidence.

CHAPTER 5

SHAPING ARGUMENTS

MODULE V-1

WHAT AUDIENCES EXPECT OF A STATE-THE-FACTS ARGUMENT

We all recognize a fact when we encounter one, don't we? A **fact** can be defined as

- information that is true,
- a statement based on irrefutable, sound logic,
- a concept that is not doubted or questioned, or
- a thing that is known to exist.

How then, you may ask, is it possible for a reasonable person to doubt a fact or call something a fact when it is clearly not? After all, a fact is a fact, right? Not exactly.

Why Are Arguments of Fact Necessary?

Nearly everyone knows humans have five senses, and many people have heard that George Washington had wooden teeth. The trouble is, neither statement of "fact" is true. In addition to the five senses, you can also sense acceleration and relative temperature. And George Washington's dentures were made of lead, ivory, and animal teeth.

It is possible to attach the word *fact* to any information or statement, but calling something a fact does not mean it is true. Generally, we accept an assertion as a fact only if it can be verified. For example, any statement about the composition of George Washington's teeth can be verified or refuted by examining the actual object or consulting an authoritative source.

When a fact or facts are in dispute, a state-the-facts argument is called for. Depending upon your purpose, you can state one fact, such as that Washington's teeth contained ivory, or you can make an argument about a set of related facts. When you present a state-the-facts argument, you are trying to persuade your audience to accept the information, statement, concept, or thing that is the subject of your argument as verifiably true.

William Bernbach, a famous advertising executive, once made the following observation:

> Facts are not enough.... Until you wrap all these facts in a talented expression to which people respond, until you cloak those facts in the artistry which makes people *feel*, you are not going to communicate.

If you want to persuade your audience of the facts you know, the facts alone are not enough, for two reasons. First, your audience has been overwhelmed with assertions of fact that turn out not to be true. For example, how often does the fast food you order look like the meal advertised? Second, facts do not speak for themselves, so you have to communicate both the fact and the fact's significance.

Reasonable people, including the doubters in your audience, will generally accept as true a fact that has been established beyond doubt, such as the fact that water boils at 212°F. Sources or reasoning that you can use to verify facts that are not as well established include reference books like *The World Almanac and Book of Facts*, respected news magazines and newspapers like *The Wall Street Journal*, and peer reviewed, academic journals.

Using Invention to Find a Context for Facts

Writers or speakers persuade and assure their audience of the truth of the facts they are presenting by providing an appropriate **context** for them. Facts need context to make them meaningful, and context is discovered and developed during research and invention. Context is not only the situation or setting in which you find facts; it is also the situation *you* create when you combine and communicate facts to your audience. In the absence of context, readers can draw the wrong conclusion from facts. Consider these well-known facts about the attack that happened in New York City on September 11, 2001, when terrorists hijacked two commercial aircraft and intentionally crashed them into the Twin Towers of the World Trade Center:

> The Twin Towers were attacked on 9/11.
> The first plane that hit a tower was Flight AA 11.
> The emergency number in New York is 911.
> New York City has an 11th Avenue and an 11th Street.
> New York State was the 11th state to join the union.
> From a distance, the towers looked like the number 11.

Each separate statement of fact is true, but combining them suggests a relationship among the facts that isn't real. If you found this list on the website *Illuminati Conspiracy Archive*, that context suggests a conspiratorial interpretation of these tragic events. However, a mathematician could explain that this list is actually an example of the "law of truly large numbers": in any large sample, such as the numerous facts about New York City, seemingly meaningful coincidences will appear as an example of synchronicity. The mathematician's explanation provides a very different context and shapes the facts differently. Though the facts remain the same, the two different contexts lead to two very different ways of understanding the list of facts.

Making Facts Acceptable to Your Audience

Your audience has no reason to believe what you believe, which is why you need to provide the **source of your facts**. Simply saying that Washington's teeth are not made of wood is not as persuasive as providing a photograph of Washington's lead and ivory dentures, identifying their current location, and including a link so readers can verify the facts themselves. In the same way, your professor is unlikely to take seriously a research paper that lacks sources or has citation errors. Even if your facts are true, your inability to identify their sources can cause your audience to question your facts.

Consider the two news stories shown in Figures 5.1 and 5.2. Both are about the National Security Agency's effort to monitor the playing of fantasy games such as World of Warcraft and Second Life. Which is more persuasive? The facts are the same in both stories. However, the second is more persuasive because the source of the facts and quotations is identified. In addition, the second story is backed by the reputation of the *New York Times*, a major news organization. As the Responsible Sourcing box entitled "The Chain of Custody" shows, when you use a credible source well, its authority transfers to your own argument.

The Times Tattler
By staff reporter
Online games might seem innocuous, but they had the potential to be a "target-rich communication network" allowing intelligence suspects "a way to hide in plain sight." Virtual games "are an opportunity!" an anonymous source declared.

Figure 5.1 In this hypothetical example, the facts are from an anonymous source, and the author is anonymous as well. Without more information about the source, the facts seem questionable.

The New York Times
By Mark Mazzetti and Justin Elliott
Online games might seem innocuous, a top-secret 2008 N.S.A. document warned, but they had the potential to be a "target-rich communication network" allowing intelligence suspects "a way to hide in plain sight." Virtual games "are an opportunity!" another 2008 N.S.A. document declared.
Published: December 9, 2013

Figure 5.2 The news comes from sources that are meticulously identified by the named authors of the article. In this case the readers are more likely to put their trust in the journalists, even though they do not know them.

Making Your Facts Authoritative

Identifying your or your source's **perspective** reinforces the authority of your statement of facts for two reasons. First, honest people can interpret the same facts, and the context in which they are presented, very differently. Second, unethical writers and speakers sometimes try to pass off misinterpretations and biased views as objective reality. **Bias** is an inclination, belief, or feeling for or against an idea, person, or group. When you acknowledge your bias, you are providing full disclosure.

Of course, having a particular perspective and bias is not necessarily bad. For most experts and scholars, bias is the result of their training in a specialized discipline. You would hope that the architect you hire to design a house would be biased in favor of following building codes and rules about the weight-bearing capability of building materials.

The degrees or certificates a person holds, or his or her job or title, often indicates the kind of bias that person will have. A specialized journal or academic text has a certain bias born of expertise as well. If you find an article published in the professional journal *Law and Human Behavior*, you can be sure it will be biased toward a legal and psychological perspective on human behavior.

Responsible Sourcing
The Chain of Custody

To protect evidence, detectives at crime scenes use gloves, sealable plastic evidence bags, and cameras to photograph evidence and the larger scene. They also keep a detailed log of where and how evidence was discovered. This approach to handling evidence, known as chain of custody, ensures that evidence presented in court is uncorrupted, that it was discovered and transported carefully, and that its source has been documented.

In the same way, ethical writers, speakers, researchers, and scholars carefully protect their research and sources. To assure your reader that your facts are beyond doubt, think of your sources as evidence that needs to be protected to be persuasive.

1. **Save everything**. Save all the documentation information you will need. Photocopy all hard-copy articles, along with the journal's title page and its table of contents page. Save copies of any electronic texts in a Word or PDF format, and be sure to indicate the name of the web publisher, date of publication, source database (if it came from that type of source), and address. Always save electronic copies in two separate locations, such as on your hard drive, in cloud storage, and on a thumb drive or other external device.

2. **Don't contaminate evidence**. Cautious detectives take care not to leave their fingerprints all over evidence and would never pick up and bag only one bullet casing while leaving the others on the ground. Similarly, researchers should not contaminate their sources by using them out of context or in a way that is contrary to the source's meaning. When quoting only part of a sentence, for instance, make sure that the entire sentence supports the point you are making, not just the part you are using.

3. **Explain what you have found**. When you integrate a source into your writing, you are like a detective explaining evidence in a courtroom. Introduce your source completely, noting what makes the source authoritative and explaining how the source is relevant to your argument. Disclose any possible bias the source may have. Quote, summarize, or paraphrase the source honestly and accurately. Finally, help your reader understand its significance and how the source supports or is related to your argument.

Genres that State the Facts

Readers and listeners look to specific genres, such as news stories or résumés, because they provide a context that gives facts meaning. Genres that state the facts are important to academic writing as well as journalism and business. As the following list shows, different genres are better suited to different purposes.

- **Accident report**: a report used to establish the facts of what led to an accident, happened during the accident, and resulted from the accident.
- **Annotated bibliography**: a list of articles, books, and artifacts about or related to a specific topic and the facts of each, in the form of a description and evaluation.
- **Lab report**: a formal account of an experiment, including the question to be answered, the procedures followed, and the full results.
- **News article**: an account of recent events that provides facts and their sources, along with background information or context.
- **Research paper**: an academic argument that uses evidence drawn from sources to support a claim.

MODULE V-2

A STATE-THE-FACTS GENRE: RESEARCH PAPER

Each academic course you will take has different requirements for research papers. Professors in different disciplines will expect you to establish contexts, use sources, and show your perspective on the facts in a different way. Nevertheless, for most research-paper assignments that call for a state-the-facts argument, you will be expected to provide data and information you have discovered through research that supports your claim—the undisputed knowledge that you have gained from examining, analyzing, and evaluating that data and information.

Lauren Glass wrote the following research paper for a college writing course. It is an example of a state-the-facts argument. In this excerpt, we see Glass using a statement of facts to set up an examination of a larger debate: Is it possible, ethical, or clinically beneficial to diagnose children as psychopaths?

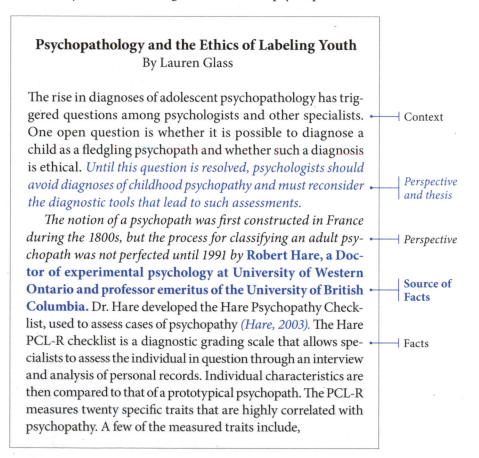

Psychopathology and the Ethics of Labeling Youth
By Lauren Glass

The rise in diagnoses of adolescent psychopathology has triggered questions among psychologists and other specialists. • ——| Context
One open question is whether it is possible to diagnose a child as a fledgling psychopath and whether such a diagnosis is ethical. *Until this question is resolved, psychologists should avoid diagnoses of childhood psychopathy and must reconsider* • ——| *Perspective and thesis*
the diagnostic tools that lead to such assessments.

The notion of a psychopath was first constructed in France during the 1800s, but the process for classifying an adult psy- • ——| *Perspective*
chopath was not perfected until 1991 by **Robert Hare, a Doctor of experimental psychology at University of Western Ontario and professor emeritus of the University of British** • ——| **Source of Facts**
Columbia. Dr. Hare developed the Hare Psychopathy Checklist, used to assess cases of psychopathy *(Hare, 2003).* The Hare
PCL-R checklist is a diagnostic grading scale that allows spe- • ——| Facts
cialists to assess the individual in question through an interview and analysis of personal records. Individual characteristics are then compared to that of a prototypical psychopath. The PCL-R measures twenty specific traits that are highly correlated with psychopathy. A few of the measured traits include,

- glib and superficial charm
- grandiose (exaggeratedly high) estimation of self
- need for stimulation
- pathological lying
- cunning and manipulativeness
- lack of remorse or guilt
- shallow affect (superficial emotional responsiveness)
- callousness and lack of empathy
- parasitic lifestyle *(Hare, 2003).* — *Source of Facts*

Each of the traits is ranked between 0 and 2, based on how well it applies to the individual being tested. A prototypical psychopath would receive a total of 40, the maximum score. A score of 30 or above qualifies a person for a diagnosis of psychopathy. People with no criminal backgrounds normally score around 5, while non-psychopathic criminal offenders score around 22 *(Hare, 2003).*

The danger of a psychopath lies predominantly in their sadistic, violent nature. Delinquent offenders with pronounced psychopathic traits display these tendencies earlier *(Brandt et al., 1997; Forth & Burke, 1998)*, commit more crimes, and engage in criminal activity more often *(Forth & Burke, 1998; Myers, 1995)* and more violently **(Brandt et al., 1997; Spain et al., 2004)** than young criminals who are not psychopathic. Psychopathy scores have also been found to correlate significantly with the severity of conduct problems, antisocial behavior, and delinquency in adolescents *(Forth & Burke, 1998).* — Facts — **Two authors of a single source**

Psychopathy has been shown to predict future violence in adults both while in prison and after discharge *(Salekin et al., 1996).* Studies of institutional violence indicate moderately strong correlations between psychopathy score and verbal and physical aggression *(Edens et al., 2001; Spain et al., 2004).* Though no checklist has yet been created for children, a version of Hare's Checklist has been created for adolescents. The checklist for adults was altered to account for the impulsivity that is characteristic of this age. Using the adolescent-adjusted PCL-R, researchers found that higher psychopathy scores in adolescents were associated with the reoccurrence of violent, undesired behaviors *(Forth et al., 1990)* and shorter intervals between episodes of these behaviors *(Brandt et al., 1997).* — Facts — Paragraphs cut for brevity

. . .

There are, however, **critics of the PCL-R such as** *Dr. Daniel Seagrave,* a **clinical and forensic psychologist** *and Dr. Thomas Grisso,* **Professor of Psychiatry, Director of Psychology, and Director of the Law-Psychiatry Program at the University of Massachusetts Medical School.** *Writing in the journal* Law and Human Behavior, *Seagrave and Grisso (2002),* **question the validity of the PCL-R, especially for adolescents.** They point out **the PCL-R was constructed for adults and has a high false-positive rate in adolescence, as this is a period of considerable developmental change.**

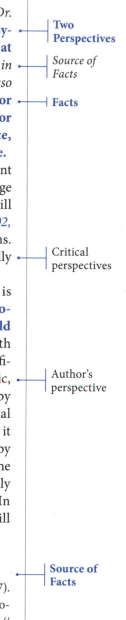

Two Perspectives

Source of Facts

Facts

Others who oppose the test and diagnosing adolescent psychopathology condemn it because of the possible damage it might inflict upon a child. Psychologists claim that it will subject children to discrimination *(Seagrave & Grisso, 2202, p. 221)* and cause them to identify with other psychopaths. The potential emotional damage would increase dramatically if the child was genuinely not psychopathic.

Critical perspectives

In spite of the risks false positive results present, it is essential to identify fledgling psychopaths. **Many psychologists are concerned with the psychological effects a child will experience if diagnosed.** Labeling affects children with other mental disorders, such as A.D.H.D. or O.C.D., significantly. However, assuming a child is indeed psychopathic, his or her mental stability will probably not be altered by this label. Since psychopaths are characterized by superficial charm, manipulativeness, and a lack of empathy and guilt, it is likely if not definite that such a child will not be upset by this diagnosis. Psychopathic youth will not fall victim to the belief that something is wrong with them. If they are truly psychopathic, they may feign an overdramatized reaction. In reality, however, their perceptions of their self-identity will not be influenced.

Author's perspective

References

Source of Facts

Brandt, J. R., Kennedy, W. A., Patrick, C. J., & Curtin, J. J. (1997). Assessment of psychopathy in a population of incarcerated adolescent offenders. *Psychological Assessment*, 9(4), 429. https://psycnet.apa.org/doi/10.1037/1040-3590.9.4.429

Edens, J. F., Skeem, J. L., Cruise, K. R., & Cauffman, E. (2001).

Assessment of "juvenile psychopathy" and its association with violence: A critical review. *Behavioral Sciences & the Law, 19*(1), 53–80. https://doi.org/10.1002/bsl.425

Forth, A. E., & Burke, H. C. (1998). Psychopathy in adolescence: Assessment, violence, and developmental precursors. In D. J. Cooke, A. E. Forth, & R. D. Hare (Eds.), *Psychopathy: Theory, research and implications for society* (pp. 205–229). Springer Netherlands.

Hare, R. D. (2003). *Manual for the revised psychopathy checklist* (2nd ed.). http://www.mhs.com/product.aspx?gr= saf&id= overview&prod=pcl-r2

Harris, H. E., Burket, R. C., & Myers, W. C. (1995). Adolescent psychopathy in relation to delinquent behaviors, conduct disorder, and personality disorders. *Journal of Forensic Science, 40*(3), 435–440. https://psycnet.apa.org/doi/10.1520/JFS13798J

Salekin, R. T., Rogers, R., & Sewell, K. W. (1996). A review and meta-analysis of the Psychopathy Checklist and Psychopathy Checklist-Revised: Predictive validity of dangerousness. *Clinical Psychology: Science and Practice, 3*(3), 203–215. https://psycnet. apa.org/doi/10.1111/j.1468-2850.1996.tb00071.x

Seagrave, D., & Grisso, T. (2002). Adolescent development and the measurement of juvenile psychopathy. *Law and human behavior, 26*(2), 219. https://doi.org/10.1023/A:1014696110850

Spain, S. E., Douglas, K. S., Poythress, N. G., & Epstein, M. (2004). The relationship between psychopathic features, violence and treatment outcome: The comparison of three youth measures of psychopathic features. *Behavioral Sciences & the Law, 22*(1), 85–102. https://doi.org/10.1002/bsl.576

APA
Style

Perspective

Perspective

Questions to Consider

Invention

1. Glass was allowed to choose any topic for this assignment. What may have prompted Glass to write about this subject?

2. Assuming that Glass is not an expert on the subject, how do you think she gathered ideas and evidence?

3. What did Glass discover about diagnosing adolescent psychopathology, and what new insights do the facts she provides give the reader?

Audience

4. To whom is Glass writing, and how do you know? .

5. Glass makes assumptions about her audience. What are these assumptions, and how do they affect the facts she presents?

6. Based on how Glass talks about the facts, what does she want her intended readers to think after they have finished reading?

Authority

7. How does Glass let the reader know what she has discovered and that her information can be trusted?

8. Which facts, if any, need further verification? Which facts with supporting sources are there, if any, that may not be accepted by the intended audience? Why not?

9. Do you accept Glass's argument, based on the facts she presents? Why or why not? What could she do to make her argument more persuasive?

MODULE V-3

WHAT AUDIENCES EXPECT OF A DEFINITION ARGUMENT

Open a local or national newspaper, and at the heart of the biggest stories you are likely to find a definition in dispute. For example, the current Israeli–Palestinian conflict rages over a definition: How are the borders of Israel and Palestine to be defined? The debate about gun control and the Second Amendment boils down to how the constitutional phrase "a well regulated militia" is defined. On a university campus, the way "hazing" is defined can mean the difference between long-lived tradition or a student-handbook violation.

Why Would I Need to Define?

In an academic setting, a definition essay is a common assignment. Such assignments may ask you to define an idea or event using existing words and classifications. In history and psychology courses, you may be expected to define terms such as "colonialism" or to explain how observations of behaviors and events fit existing definitions or classifications. In a composition or writing class you may be asked to write a personal definition—what a word, phrase, or idea such as "social justice" means to you.

Because so much depends on definitions, a definitional argument needs to be clear, decisive, and based on evidence. Persuasive definitional arguments redefine an existing word or argue for a new word and new definition. Therefore, you must take a position by explaining why the previous definition should be replaced and why a new definition is necessary, or by persuading the audience that the new word and its definition are accurate, insightful, and better than other possibilities.

Types of Definitions

To **define** is to state the meaning or meanings of a word or phrase, establish the boundaries or extent of a word or phrase, designate the qualities or characteristics that a word or phrase refers to, and resolve misunderstandings about a word's or phrase's meaning. Whenever you are trying to persuade someone to think or act differently, you are probably going to use a definition or make a definitional argument. Because definitions are the building blocks of opinions and persuasive arguments, tradition provides you with different types of definitions. Knowing which type to use based on your purpose and your intended audience will help you build a persuasive argument.

Formal Definition

A **formal definition** describes the range of qualities and characteristics that differentiate the word or phrase from other similar examples. To make a formal definition, the word to be defined is first placed in a larger class or category of things or ideas with similar qualities and characteristics. For example, an oak tree can be placed in the larger category of trees. The formal definition then shows how the word to be defined, like "oak," is different from all other things and ideas within the larger group "tree":

Larger class

Word defined — An oak is a type of **tree** that **has hard** wood and **leaves arranged** spirally around a branch. An oak can grow up to **80 feet tall**, produces acorns, and has a **light grayish bark.** — Distinguishing characteristic

When people look a word up in a dictionary, they expect to find a formal definition. Formal definitions can appear in any type of argument, but they are exceptionally useful in arguments of analysis and evaluation, where you must compare one object or idea with others in a larger class. For example, you could argue that alternative rap (the phrase to be defined) does not get the airplay of other types of hip-hop music (larger class) because it blends and borrows from genres not commonly associated with hip-hop culture such as country, electronica, and folk music (distinguishing qualities). The Conventions in Context box entitled "Common Mistakes in Formal Definitions" will help you build a persuasive definition. For more on arguments of analysis and evaluation, see Modules V-7 and V-8.

Conventions in Context
Common Mistakes in Formal Definitions

For a formal definition to be effective, it needs to follow the structure readers expect.

The word must belong to a larger class: the word you define cannot be its own larger class. For example, you can't say an oak tree is a type of oak tree. Such a class would be too small, as it would not contain any similar, comparable trees you could use to distinguish an oak.

The class must contain comparable items: your larger class must contain comparable or similar objects or ideas. Therefore, you can't say an oak tree is a type of wood. Trees are composed of wood, but a larger class of trees does not also include types of lumber.

The class cannot be too big: you could say an oak tree is a type of living organism. However, distinguishing an oak from all other organisms, a gigantic class, would take a great deal of energy and time.

The definition must be precise: the word or phrase must be distinct from all other examples in the larger class or category. For example, the following definition describes a meter and other forms of measurement: a meter is a type of metric measurement divisible by numerations of 100. This definition fails because it can also define a liter—a measure of volume or capacity.

A good definition is built on qualities, characteristics, comparisons, and differences. If the building blocks of a definition are faulty, so too is the definition.

Operational Definition

An **operational definition** describes how a thing or idea affects the environment, is observed or measured, or is the result of a process.

For example, an NBA three-point shot is a shot made from behind a line marking an arc with a radius 23 feet 9 inches from a point directly under the basket. Go to any NBA court or watch any NBA game and you will find the same operational definition.

Operational definitions are well suited to state-the-facts arguments, cause-and-effect arguments, or any argument where you clarify or establish exact qualities or characteristics of a thing or idea. If you were to argue that global warming is due to human activity, you would first have to establish an operational definition of "human climate disruption." You might say that human-based climate disruption is defined as 440 parts per million of CO_2 in the atmosphere measured over a five-year period. For more on state-the-facts arguments and cause-and-effect arguments, see Modules V-1 and V-5.

Extensional Definition

In an **extensional definition**, every part of an object or idea is identified. For example, a "s'more" is composed of graham crackers, a chocolate bar, and a toasted marshmallow. Extensional definitions are not appropriate for objects with many parts, such as the universe, or abstract concepts, such as love.

Extensional definitions are helpful in arguments in which you need to break a big idea into smaller parts, such as cause-and-effect arguments and arguments that propose a solution. If you argue that NCAA rules about amateurism are unfair to college athletes, you might describe all the parts of the NCAA's amateurism policy and explain how each part hurts athletes or denies them opportunities. Cause-and-effect arguments are discussed in Modules V-5 and V-6, and arguments that propose a solution are discussed in Modules V-9 and V-10.

Definition by Example

A **definition by example** presents similar words, ideas, or examples that have a specific quality or trait in common with the word, phrase, or idea to be defined. If you wanted to define a *Cajon*, for instance, you could point to different examples of the instrument (see Figure 5.3).

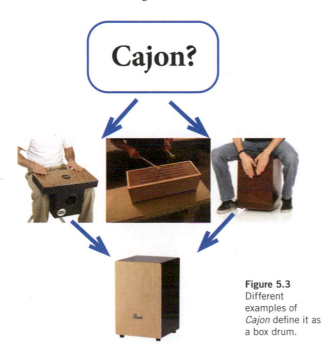

Figure 5.3
Different examples of *Cajon* define it as a box drum.

A definition by example highlights several traits or qualities, making it useful when defining a complex or abstract idea. Example definitions are useful in any persuasive argument and are often found in literary and rhetorical analysis arguments. For instance, if you wanted to argue that Jack London's short story "To Build a Fire" is an example of the naturalist literary movement, you would first define naturalism by identifying common traits or qualities of other naturalist short stories, and then show these same qualities in London's story.

Etymological Definition

An **etymological definition** shows the derivation or origin of a word and traces changes in its meaning over time. The contemporary word "cure" has Latin (*cura*) and Old French origins. Over time, it has been used to describe the care of souls (fourteenth century), the act of covering or concealing (fifteenth century), a medical treatment (seventeenth century), and an odd person (nineteenth century). Authoritative etymological definitions can be found in the *Oxford English Dictionary*.

Rhetorical analyses and determinations of cause (Module V-5) are just two of the argument forms that use etymological definitions. For example, if you wanted to persuade people to avoid websites and discussion boards where contributors write extreme, racist, or sexist posts, you might remind your audience of the etymology of the word "troll": "In the early seventeenth century, a troll was a foul-smelling, ugly dwarf or giant with big ears and a menacing disposition who lived in dark caves or under bridges and harassed passersby. Feeding trolls, whether supernatural or electronic, is never a good idea."

Using Invention to Find a Reason to Define

There are many reasons or purposes for defining or redefining a word. During invention, try out different purposes to see how they support different types of arguments. Let's consider five different reasons for defining and the kinds of arguments they can help you build.

1. **Propose a better definition**. In this case, you are arguing that the definition you propose is more appropriate to the current setting and usage, is closer to the original meaning, or is a necessary update of a current word.
   - You can define by establishing the best, most precise word for the thing, idea, person, or event you are describing. For example, the word "amateur" may no longer apply to student-athletes who get scholarships and a paycheck, and "student worker" is too general. A more accurate word may be "athletic worker."
   - You can define by returning a word to an older, previous definition. For example, "random" used to mean arbitrary or unplanned. Now it is used to

suggest something odd or strange. You might argue that people should go back to using the word "random" to mean unplanned or haphazard.

- You can redefine by pointing out that a word's meaning has shifted in common usage or among a group. For example, for many, a "friend" is someone you like and trust. However, 2.9 billion Facebook users understand "friend" as a verb, and they can "friend" people they do not know.

2. **Challenge an existing definition**. You can challenge a definition of a word by inventing alternative definitions or researching other larger classes or sets in which the word fits. When you challenge an existing definition of a word, you are also often challenging its use in a discussion or debate. The Supreme Court and gun-rights activists interpret the phrase "a well regulated militia" in the Second Amendment of the Constitution to mean private citizens who may be called upon to act as a militia. Gun-control activists challenge this definition and argue that the Constitution's framers intended "militia" to mean professional soldiers only. A change in the accepted definition—for example, by changing the larger class to which militias belong—could change the debate.

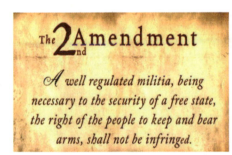

Figure 5.4
The wording of the Second Amendment to the US Constitution.

3. **Create a new word and definition**. Sometimes a new development in society or technology requires a name and a definition for that name. For example, Richard Dawkins first used and defined the word "meme" in his 1976 book *The Selfish Gene*. According to Dawkins, a "meme" is an idea, cultural trait, or behavior whose movement within a population is similar to that of a virus.

4. **Add a new element or idea to an existing definition**. In 2013, the Supreme Court struck down the federal law barring recognition of same-sex marriages. As a result, the legal definition of "marriage" now includes same-sex wedded unions, which were previously excluded.

5. **Help readers better understand words and ideas**. Definitions can inform an audience and, by doing so, establish common ground or agreement. For example, before anyone would buy an NFT or invest in "bitcoin," they must first understand what each is. In other words, these two concepts are a mystery until they are defined.

Making Your Definition Reasonable and Acceptable to Your Audience

Keep in mind that your audience may be inclined to resist your definition. In any debate about diets and food production, some vegetarians may be sympathetic to the redefinition in the phrase "meat is murder." However, if you are trying to persuade those whose diet includes cold cuts, redefining "meat" as "murder" will simply mark you as unreasonable. Modifying or adding to the definition of "meat" as "a source of protein that requires twice as much energy to produce as other proteins" is more likely to strike even a doubtful audience as a reasonable statement.

In order to determine what will be acceptable or reasonable to your audience, you will need to consider their disposition toward and current beliefs about the word or phrase you are defining. You will also need to determine what your audience might find silly or self-serving.

For example, some might be sympathetic to the Dairy Council's argument that people should think of ice cream as a post-workout protein food (Figure 5.5). But it is just as likely that some will see this definition as a clever way to increase ice-cream sales.

Figure 5.5 Is ice cream a healthy choice?

Making Your Definition Complete and Authoritative

Understandably, your audience has beliefs about how a definition works, questions about the need for defining or redefining a word they think they know, and expectations about the insight necessary to justify a redefinition or a new word altogether. In other words, first you need to establish your authority—prove you know how to define—and then you need to persuade your audience of the benefit or insight of your definition or redefinition. Only then will your audience give up their old definition and accept your argument.

Effective definitions provide insight, a new understanding and clearer vision of the subject, and persuasive definitions often illustrate this insight with examples. Defining muscle pain as soreness provides no new understanding or insight, for example. However, if your trainer defines pain as the process of weakness leaving the body, she may have just given you a new way to think about your workout. If she adds a visual example of a muscle with micro-tears that grows bigger and stronger as it heals, her insight may persuade you to work harder. The Responsible Sourcing box entitled "The Dictionary Trap" will help you avoid less than insightful definitions.

Responsible Sourcing
The Dictionary Trap

Obviously, dictionary definitions are useful during research or as the source of a definition you will redefine in your argument. However, building an argument around a dictionary definition or relying heavily upon what a dictionary says about a word can be a trap.

General dictionaries available in print or online, like the *Merriam-Webster's Collegiate Dictionary*, are helpful primarily for settling debates and checking spelling. If your professor has assigned you a definition essay, however, she is probably expecting you to pull together different sources with different perspectives to develop a coherent, insightful definition of your own. Because of these expectations, a dictionary definition will appear to be an uninspired choice. After all, if readers or listeners can look up the definition in a dictionary, what do they need you for?

If you are tempted to begin an essay with or otherwise use a definition drawn from a general dictionary, ask yourself the following:

- What does my reader expect?
- What does the definition provide that is insightful?
- What does the dictionary definition do that I couldn't do?

A professor is likely to view a citation for a dictionary definition as a shortcut that indicates a lack of mental effort.

Genres that Define

Nearly all genres of argument make use of definitions. The following genres focus primarily or typically on persuading an audience to accept a definition of a word, phrase, or idea.

- A **commercial** usually serves to define a new product or service or redefine a product or service.
- **Committee by-laws** define the identity, purpose, duties, and rights of a committee or other type of group.

- A **diagnostic manual** used by physicians defines illnesses and symptoms.
- An **opinion piece** is a short, journalistic argument in which the author tries to persuade the audience of her or his opinion.
- A **research paper** can redefine existing knowledge by describing new discoveries and new knowledge.
- A **review of scholarly literature** defines the subject of articles and books.

MODULE V-4

A DEFINITION GENRE: RESEARCH PAPER

For her final Honors seminar, Cedar Smith explored the science of happiness. She looked to psychologists and experts to better understand why some people are consistently happy while others are not. The excerpt below is her first step—persuade her audience to reconsider their understanding of *moods*, a central term in the current research of happiness, and the relationship of moods to well-being.

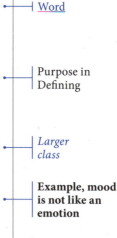

An Ever-Changing State: What the Science of Happiness Can Teach Us about Our Moods

If someone asked you to describe your current <u>mood</u>, most likely you would have an instant response. You know exactly how you feel, and you are probably aware that mood influences every second of your life. Few of us think about mood or what a mood is. Yet <u>mood</u> is related to other parts of your life; it shapes your experiences and outlook and can affect your mental health and general well-being.

⊣ Word

| Purpose in Defining

To explore and understand <u>mood</u>, we must first define it. When we think of moods, we think of *emotions, of feelings, of attitude, of sentiment.* Generally, a <u>mood</u> is **a temporary feeling marked by an overriding emotion or sentiment.** However, a <u>mood</u> is **not simply an emotion like sadness, which is typically provoked by an event and is specific, intense, and focused. A mood is less intense and may not be provoked by anything, and yet** <u>moods</u> are powerful.

| *Larger class*

| **Example, mood is not like an emotion**

| **Distinguishing characteristic**

As William Morris and Paula Schnurr, the authors of *Mood: The Frame of Mind*, have noted, <u>moods</u> **"are capable of altering**

| **Distinguishing characteristic**

our affective, cognitive, and behavioral responses to a wide array of objects and events" (2). Think back to a time when you were in what would be labeled as a bad mood. Most likely, you had no desire to interact with people, maybe you wanted to be left alone, or were angry and had no urge to engage in your favorite activities. Moods can change your perspective, your desires, and your thoughts. And moods can wreak havoc on individuals' lives. From Major Depressive Disorder, Generalized Anxiety Disorder, Seasonal Affective Disorder, and Bipolar Disorder, these disturbances in moods are major psychological problems that impede and affect the lives of many.

MLA in-text citation

Example, mood is like this

Distinguishing characteristic

Moods can be understood as positive and negative. A positive mood is difficult to define, but in its essence it is a general feeling of well-being. We can use the terms happy mood and positive mood interchangeably; as Sonja Lyubomirsky explains in her book *The How of Happiness: A Scientific Approach to Getting the Life You Want*, "the hallmark of happiness, feelings of joy, delight, contentment, vigor, thrill, curiosity, interest, serenity, and pride" are the same aspects of positive moods (258).

Distinguishing characteristic

Distinguishing characteristic

Lyubomirsky cites a number of studies that show that "happy moods, no matter the source, lead people to be more productive, more likable, more active, more healthy, more friendly, more helpful, more resilient, and more creative" (258). So how can we experience a positive mood for ourselves? The science of happiness tells us that expressing gratitude, savoring experiences, and laughter are all things that can put us in a positive mood.

New Insight

On the other side are negative moods. A negative mood is a state of tension, nervousness, worry, anger, guilt, sadness, self-dissatisfaction, and/or distress. People may attribute negative moods to unstable and uncontrollable external events or internal enduring aspects of self (Morris and Schnurr 151). The things that put us in a negative mood are similar to if not the same as the things that bring us out of a happy mood, notably, complaining and ruminating.

Distinguishing characteristic

New Insight

MLA in-text citation

As the research shows, a mood is not a feeling or simply an emotion, but a long term cognitive state that can shape the way we experience events, express ourselves, and can

New Insight

even change the way we think and interact with the world. Now that we understand moods more deeply, let's look at what cognitive psychologists have discovered about our ability to alter or effect our own mood and the moods of others....

Works Cited

Lyubomirsky, Sonja. *The How of Happiness: A Scientific Approach to Getting the Life You Want.* Penguin Press, 2008.

Morris, William N., and Paula P. Schnurr. *Mood: The Frame of Mind.* Springer-Verlag, 1989.

MLA style Works Cited

Questions to Consider

Invention

1. In the excerpt above, what is Smith's purpose?

2. Since Smith is not an expert, she needed to rely on invention and research to help her establish an authoritative voice. What do you imagine were her first and second steps when inventing?

3. What types of definitions are used in this excerpt from Smith's research paper about mood? How do they contribute to your understanding of the word or idea being defined?

Audience

4. Often, Smith appears to talk directly to her audience by posing questions. How does such an approach affect her readers and their view of the author?

5. What does Smith assume her readers think about mood before they read her argument, and what does she want readers to think, believe, or do after they have finished?

6. Smith makes assumptions about what her audience knows and thinks. Where do you see Smith using these assumptions to build her definition?

Authority

7. How does Smith let her readers know that her definitions are accurate and can be trusted?

8. Where in the definition did you wish you had more context or background? Why?

9. By the end, do you have a good understanding of the concept of mood? What more do you need to know to accept the definition or to make your understanding complete?

MODULE V-5

WHAT AUDIENCES EXPECT OF A CAUSAL ARGUMENT

An argument that defines and explains the cause of an effect or traces the effects of a cause is called a **causal argument**. In addition, arguments that disprove or dispute causes or effects are also causal. Often, knowledge cannot advance until a faulty belief in a cause or an effect is disproven.

Academic disciplines and many professions have specialized means of looking for causes and effects. In fact, causal arguments are the foundation of most academic discussions and everyday debates.

Figure 5.6
Doctors did not stop bloodletting until it was proven that an imbalance of the humors (blood, bile, and phlegm) was not the cause of illness.

Why Would I Need to Write about Cause and Effect?

Making an argument that identifies cause and effect is not as simple as declaring that one thing caused another. As a student, if you are asked why a poet chose a specific rhyme scheme, why in 1890 the US frontier was said to be closed, or what chemical effect Mentos candy has on diet soda, you should be prepared to respond with an argument that persuasively describes causes and effects based on evidence. An effective causal argument persuades the audience by helping readers understand the relationship between a cause and an effect.

As you learn how a discipline generates and discovers knowledge, you will also see how it deals with cause and effect. The Conventions in Context box provides some examples.

Conventions in Context
Cause and Effect in Academic Disciplines

Different academic disciplines use cause and effect arguments in different ways.

Sciences: The scientific method, in which we make observations, form a hypothesis about what we see, experiment to test the hypothesis, and then revise it, is a system that distinguishes between correlations (simple links between events or data points, without evidence of a causal connection) and situations where one data point or event is altered or caused by another. For example, a scientist who measures higher global temperatures also observes increases of atmospheric CO_2 over the same time period. However, this correlation does not mean the increase in CO_2 actually causes higher global temperatures. Scientists must do experiments to prove or disprove the hypothesis that higher levels of CO_2 cause higher global temperatures.

Theology: One causal argument is the first-cause argument for the existence of God, who in this argument is the prime mover and first cause of all actions and changes in the universe. In this argument, take away God and you take away all subsequent effects and events.

Engineering: Engineers consider closed systems, like electronic circuits, and examine the effects caused by various inputs. For example, an engineer may input static electricity to a circuit to see how the materials and function of the circuit change.

Law: To establish guilt, a lawyer must prove to the jury that there is a causal link between the accused person's actions and the crime. For a lawyer to link you to a hit-and-run accident involving a UPS truck, she would have to prove that the smudge of brown paint on your car was caused by a collision with the truck. However, if you can prove an alternative causal link, such as that your brown garage door scraped your fender and left a smudge, you can create doubt about the lawyer's causal argument.

Types of Cause-and-Effect Relationships

A cause can be categorized in three different ways, and the evidence required to prove each type of cause differs.

1. A **sufficient cause** is all that is required for an effect to occur. For example, an enormous increase in static charges in a cloud is sufficient—it is enough—to cause lightning.

   The sufficient cause of lightning is a large static charged cloud. A sufficient cause is the strongest link between cause and effect, so it requires undeniable evidence to be persuasive.

2. A **necessary cause** is one of many causes of an effect. For example, heat, often in the form of lightning, is a necessary cause of fire, but heat by itself is not enough to cause a fire, just as lightning does not always cause a fire. To cause a fire, heat, oxygen, and fuel (like wood) must be present.

   Fire has three necessary causes—heat, oxygen, and fuel.

   A single necessary cause is not enough to establish a cause-and-effect relationship. To form a strong link to an effect, all necessary causes must be explained. Because necessary causes merely contribute to an effect, their relationship to the effect is not as strong as that of a sufficient cause.

3. A **contributory cause** is one of many causes that can be linked to an effect, but it is neither necessary nor sufficient. Underground mining can contribute to minor earthquakes; however, it is not a necessary cause because there are many reasons for earthquakes, and it is not a sufficient cause because many mines operate for years without earthquake activity. Because it is only contributory, the persuasive force of this type of cause is modest compared to proven sufficient or necessary causes.

If you have found a cause-and-effect relationship, it is one of these three, which means you do not need to invent a new way of characterizing the cause-and-effect relationship you are exploring.

Now that you understand how causes are related to effects, you are ready to explore how causal arguments are structured.

Using Invention to Structure a Causal Argument

Causal arguments can be structured in three basic ways:

- an argument that starts with a cause and links to an effect,
- a causal chain argument, and
- an argument that starts with an effect and links to a cause.

A strong thesis often mirrors the structure of the argument that follows. Below, you will find three ways to structure a thesis and its supporting arguments.

1. Argument that Starts with a Cause and Links to an Effect

> [**X cause(s)**] → [**Y effect(s)**]

The increase in the minimum wage has caused entry-level jobs to disappear in our area.

The simplest versions of this structure allow you to argue that a cause or a
number of causes are linked to one or more effects.

You can also use this simple structure to invent an argument that disagrees
with a causal claim made by someone else, and then argue for a different effect.
The ¬ symbol is used by logicians to indicate negation or "not."

> [**X cause(s)**] ¬ [**Y effect(s)**]
> [**X cause(s)**] → [**Z effect(s)**]

The increase in the minimum wage did not eliminate entry-level jobs
in our area. Instead, the wage hike reduced turnover in entry-level jobs.

An argument that moves from a cause to an effect always looks forward, since
causes always come before effects.

2. Causal Chain Argument

> [**X cause(s)**] → [**Y effect(s)**] → [**Y cause(s)**] → [**Z effect(s)**]

The first car skidded, which caused the second car to hit the first car,
which caused the third car to hit the second car.

A causal chain argument claims that two or more effects are linked and that
the sequence was set in motion by a first cause or causes.

A strong causal-chain argument requires careful research and solid reasoning. Different people will have different perceptions of the same events, which
is why the person making this argument must prove the first causal link, elim-
inating other possibilities, before moving on to the next effect in the sequence.

3. Argument that Starts with an Effect and Links to a Cause

> [**Y effect(s)**] ← [**X cause(s)**]

The militarization of police tactics is an effect of the military equipment
in their inventory.

This structure starts with an effect or effects and describes its cause or multiple causes. Arguments from effect to cause can include multiple effects brought about by multiple causes.

In addition, you can use this structure to dispute the cause or causes proposed by someone else. For example,

[Y effect(s)] ← [W cause(s)] ¬ [X cause(s)]

The militarization of police tactics are an effect of military methods and practices used to train police officers, and not an effect of the military equipment in their inventory.

Until you do the research to discover all possible effects, you can't be sure you know what happened. In addition, if you do not consider all possible explanations for the effects you see, you will not find the evidence to persuade your audience of the cause you argue for.

Making Your Causal Argument Acceptable to Your Audience

The most basic expectation of a causal argument is that the writer will answer the *why*, *how*, and *what* questions. Why did the event or change happen? How is the cause related to the effects? What are the effects?

Answers to the *why* question often begin with the word *because*—the conjunction indicating causality. When arguing for a cause, keep in mind that your audience may think that a different cause is more likely. After all, there is no point in building a causal argument for an audience that already thinks as you do. Therefore, you cannot simply identify a cause and move on to its effects. You need to consider other possible causes and then eliminate them with evidence. Finally, you must use evidence and reasoning to prove the cause you are arguing for is the most likely.

When your audience asks *how*, one of the three types of cause-and-effect relationships is the answer. Each type of cause-and-effect relationship has a different level of persuasive force, and not every type will support every argument. For example, if you are arguing that fracking in Oklahoma must be shut down to prevent further earthquakes, those who benefit from the 100-million-barrel Oklahoma oilfields will require evidence proving that fracking is a sufficient or one of a few necessary causes of recent earthquakes. A contributory cause argument simply will not persuade oil producers. Obviously, the type of cause-and-effect relationship you argue for must come from the data and events you analyze, and without evidence and solid reasoning you can't establish a cause-and-effect relationship.

When you focus on the effects and their consequences, you answer the "what happened or what resulted" question. Because a cause always precedes an effect, you must persuade your audience of the cause and its relationship to the effect or effects before they will accept your thesis that the effect or effects you are arguing for result from a specific cause. Audiences will expect answers to the *why, how,* and *what* questions. If you have the answers, you are ready to make your argument more authoritative than competing arguments.

Breaking the Block
Using Stasis Questions to Find Causes and Effects

Stasis questions of cause and consequence can help you look deeper. The goal of this exercise is to find a subject for a causal argument in the form of a research paper. The writing component of this exercise should take 10 minutes.

Step One
Search the news for events whose cause or effect is debated, for example, the effect of a candidate's economic platform or the cause of an accident. If nothing jumps out at you, the following prompts can help you find a causal issue.

- Name three events that are well known or common, like an injury at a music festival, the election of an unlikely candidate, or the sinking of a ship.
- Think of a plan, scheme, or trip in your experience that ended badly or had unexpected consequences.
- List all the machines, devices, or appliances you've owned that stopped working or malfunctioned for no obvious reason.
- Look at things you handle or see every day, like your smartphone. What effect does the shape or functions have on you?
- Think about purposes or final outcomes. For example, what is the purpose of body armor and helmets worn by police? Are they only to protect, or do they send a message? What are the effects of mega-amusement parks on the surrounding environment?

Step Two
Choose the most interesting or confusing events, changes, or final outcomes and write for 10 minutes developing answers to the following secondary stasis questions.

- Why did an event or change happen?
- How are the possible causes and possible effects of an event or changes related?

- What are the possible effects?
- What possible causes or effects do not make sense or can be eliminated?
- What was the immediate or most obvious effect?
- What other consequences will become apparent later or in other locations or situations?

Step Three
Reflect upon what you have written. Could reasonable people point to other causes or effects? What would they base their contrary conclusions on? How could you prove your observations or theory?

Making Your Causal Argument Authoritative

Building authority is a matter of using logical reasoning to help your reader understand the evidence that supports your argument. Like showing your work in a math class, if your audience can follow your reasoning, checking accuracy if need be, and then come up with the same conclusion you do, you have demonstrated your authority.

Your audience will recognize your authority, or not, in the way in which you answer the *why*, *how*, and *what* questions. For example, if someone argued that last week's earthquake in Logan County was caused by the fracking rig that started operation in the county two weeks ago, that person could be making a ***post hoc ergo propter hoc*** fallacy. The *post hoc* fallacy is an overestimation of the significance of a sequence of events. Just because fracking preceded an earthquake does not prove it caused the earthquake.

If someone had undeniable evidence that a fracking rig drilling and pumping high-pressure liquid into a fault did in fact cause last week's earthquake, however, he or she would be making a hasty generalization by then arguing that all Oklahoma earthquake swarms are an effect of fracking. A **hasty generalization** fallacy is an overestimation of the significance of the sample size or number of observations made. One observation (sample size of 1) of a single fracking-caused earthquake does not prove the cause of all earthquakes in Oklahoma. Many more observations (a greater sample size) are required to support such a conclusion.

Reasoning is persuasive but evidence is convincing, and direct evidence is stronger than circumstantial or indirect evidence. To understand the difference, imagine that as you wake up in the morning you hear the pitter patter of falling water and smell cool, fresh air drifting through your bedroom window. If you conclude, as you leave for work, that a rain shower is the cause of your wet bike seat, your argument is based on circumstantial or indirect evidence. **Circumstantial or indirect evidence** is evidence that requires an inference or interpretation to connect a cause to an effect.

You have no direct evidence of rain, but you are inferring that the rain happened because you experienced the sound of falling water and a wet bike seat. **Direct evidence**, on the other hand, is undeniable evidence that directly supports your conclusion, such as actually seeing raindrops fall from the overcast sky onto your bike.

Audiences judge your authority by the reasoning and evidence you use. Module II-6 will help you evaluate the persuasive power of evidence.

Genres that Determine Cause

A cause-and-effect argument can be one part of a larger argument or paper. Below is a brief list of genres that make use of causal arguments and often consist primarily of causal arguments.

- A **lab report** is the record of a completed experiment, including the original hypothesis that predicts causes and effects.
- A **closing argument** is a restatement of arguments in a courtroom, with a lawyer describing the guilt or innocence, or liability or lack of responsibility, of a defendant in a court case.
- A **historical analysis** is an examination of historical events and artifacts to determine cause-and-effect relationships between individuals, acts, ideas, and events.
- A **political cartoon** expresses a political view for the purpose of persuading the audience.
- An **editorial** is a short journalistic argument in which the author tries to persuade the audience to think, believe, or act differently.
- A **research paper** can argue for a new understanding by offering a thesis about a possible cause-and-effect relationship, backed by credible evidence.

MODULE V-6

A CAUSAL ARGUMENT GENRE: RESEARCH PAPER

In the following essay for a psychology course, entitled "Resilience and Development," student Elicia Flemming examines the causes of identity development and then argues that educational institutions must understand and respond to the stressors that can inhibit academic success.

Assessing the Desire for Success: How Bi-Cultural Identity Development Strains Academic Motivation in Immigrant Youth
Elicia Flemming

Immigration shapes America. The population of immigrants is increasing at a rapid rate, and by 2040, one-third of all children will be growing up in immigrant households (Suárez-Orozco et al., 2010). Unfortunately, two-thirds of the immigrant population experience steady declines in academic performance during their education while another fourteen percent of immigrants are labeled as low achievers from the start of their academic careers (Suárez-Orozco et al., 2010).

Introduction of scope and focus

To assist immigrants on their paths towards academic success, schools and colleges must be aware of and respond to the psychological stresses that challenge identity development and academic achievement. In this paper, I argue that the challenges of successfully developing a bi-cultural identity negatively affect immigrant academic achievement and personal development.

Thesis

During the process of assimilating into American culture, immigrant adolescents are faced with the challenge of maintaining the values of their home culture while simultaneously attempting to assimilate into their new culture (Rodriguez et al., 2003). This dual-sided development of identity provides a consistent source of pressure for **new immigrants who are essentially undergoing the process of assuming new identities in America.** Understanding the process and pressures working against positive identity formation can help educators and society ease immigrant academic success and assimilation.

General cause challenging identity development

Identity development— the general effect

Jacquelynne Eccles' theory of Expectancy Value Perspective explains that **positive identity formation is an effect** of *three linked causes: positive personal motivation, participation in socially appropriate behaviors, and realistic personal assessment.* Motivation is, perhaps, the most important of the three, because without it the other two causes are unlikely.

General cause composed of a three part causal chain

Positive motivation is tied to positive acts. An individual must first be motivated to identify new and different activities

First linked cause

and actions they are willing and able to complete and then they must behave, over time, in a way that corresponds with these motivations (Eccles, 2000). In the context of academic perfor-mance, students who are motivated to excel must first identify new behaviors that will contribute to their social success. **For example, in the original culture, an immigrant may have been labeled a good student if he or she sat silently and did not disrupt the class with talking. Such behaviors, which the immigrant mastered and grew comfortable with, may be inappropriate in an American academic context. Motivation in academic setting often means a willingness to put oneself in new, uncomfortable situations and try activities that the student has not yet mastered.**

Motivation is necessary, but not sufficient to positive iden-tity formation, especially in academic situations. *A student must also engage in socially appropriate behaviors. If students are motivated to behave in a way that corresponds to socially appropriate behaviors,* **they are essentially forming an iden-tity as a good student. A willingness to try new activities and practice new behaviors is also tied to the third cause, which is the ability to assess one's own skills and abilities.**

Eccles explains that *self-perceptions of personal skills and competencies shape how successful an individual perceives he or she will be. This awareness, in combination with perceptions related to goals that are shaped by a larger social context, allows an individual to assess the value of the behavior in relation to the social context.* **For example, motivated immigrant stu-dents who have learned how to behave in class and take part in appropriate behaviors learn over time how to judge their own work and compare their efforts to those of their classmates. As a result, when a student receives praise for hard work, he or she is likely to repeat the same study habits on the next assignment. If a student sees that his or her in-class work habits and participation are less than the work and participation of praised students, that student is likely to study more or ask for help—another form of positive participation in appropriate behaviors.**

Expectancy Value Perspective theory demonstrates that motivation, an understanding of appropriate behaviors, and

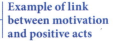

Example of link between motivation and positive acts

Effect of motivation

Second linked cause

Effect of participation is socially appropriate acts

Link between first, second, third necessary cause

Third cause of positive identity formation

Example of causal link

Summary of Eccles research

having positive ideas about being successful in combination with the values of the larger social context are essential to identity formation for immigrant students (Eccles, 2000). **Unfortunately, the chain of causes that result in positive identity development can be strained or disrupted by particular challenges associated with immigrant status.** Because the majority of America's immigrants have *low-socioeconomic status and often reside in urban, poverty stricken areas, these particular contexts may not promote educational success.* **Latino immigrants, for example, place more significance on their interpersonal relationships with family, extended family, and members of the community (Rodriguez et al., 2003). If the family values finding a job as more important than getting good grades in school,** motivation for academic achievement will be unsupported and is likely to disappear. In this way, the student's emphasis on family may override conflicting notions of what is valued in the dominant school-group setting.

Immigrants also face stressors and impediments that may keep them from participating in socially appropriate behaviors that contribute to positive identity development. *Immigrants experience stressors related to exclusion, which are "the institutional barriers of acceptance and inclusion in the culture and economy of our nation" (Roffman et al., 2003). This institutional barrier sends implicit messages about who belongs in the context of American culture and who doesn't.*

Institutions are not the only source of exclusionary behaviors that stress immigrant students. When studying the academic performance of blacks and Latinos in school settings, Reynolds and Beehler found that *the psychological distress caused by being a victim of individual racism, or being exposed to racism, positively correlated with intrinsic motivation and participation (Reynolds & Beehler, 2010). In this way, the psychological distress that is caused by being negatively targeted or judged on the basis of race or immigrant status causes a lack of achievement in school.*

Conflict between cultures makes the process of assessing strengths and weakness more difficult. For immigrants, identi-

Causal chain easily broken

Cause leading to lower academic achievement

Example of causal link breakdown

Negative effect of break in causal chain

Institutions may limit or inhibit participation

Individual racism also a cause

fying in what ways they are successful may be more challenging when they are in a new, unfamiliar environment. Unfortunately, the social setting immigrant children are surrounded by may also assist in setting up personal expectations for failure among youth. Peers, school administrators, teachers, community members, and the media often stereotype them as lazy, irresponsible, unintelligent, and dangerous. Such stereotypes negatively shift immigrant perspectives on their ability to achieve success within this social context (Roffman et al., 2003). **The critical process of identity development involved with assessing personal strengths is disrupted because of the individual's difficulty in accurately viewing his or her strengths and weaknesses in a different, sometimes harsh country.**

Stereotypes and low societal expectations a cause

Effect of stereotypes and low expectations

Despite the stressors and the difficulties, the development of a bicultural identity results in substantial benefits. **Students who successfully overcome the challenges of this identity communicate more easily with friends, make friends with students from other academic backgrounds, and achieve a higher amount of academic success** (Suárez-Orozco et al., 2010).

Positive effects of causal chain

In conclusion, immigrant adolescents face a far more difficult time than their nonimmigrant peers. Due to the amount of academic decline that is observed within the immigrant culture, it is critical that our educational institutions pay attention to and accommodate the psychological distress and challenges that lead to low academic performance. If immigrant youth are provided with resources that ease the formation of a bi-cultural identity and help undo the increased psychological distress that they experience, we will begin to witness positive feelings of belonging within the context of American culture and positive perceptions for the future. When positive outlooks are achieved, immigrant youth will be more motivated to excel in school and will break past the barriers that limit their success in America.

Summary and final appeal

References

Eccles, J. (2000). Who am I and what am I going to do with my life? Personal and collective identities as motivators of action. *Educational Psychologist*, 44(2), 78–89. https://psycnet.apa.org/doi/10.1080/00461520902832368

APA citations

Reynolds, A. L., Sneva, J. N., & Beehler, G. P. (2010). The influence of racism-related stress on the academic motivation of Black and Latino/a students. *Journal of College Student Development*, *51*(2), 135–149. https://psycnet.apa.org/doi/10.1353/csd.0.0120

Rodriguez, M. C., Morrobel, D., & Villarruel, F. A. (2003). Research realities and a vision of success for Latino youth development. In F. Villarruel, D. Perkins, L. Borden, & J. Keith (Eds.), *Community Youth Development: Programs, Policies, and Practices* (pp. 47–78). Sage Publications.

Roffman, J. G., Suárez-Orozco, C., & Rhodes, J. E. (2003). Facilitating positive youth development in immigrant youth: The role of mentors and community organizations. In F. Villarruel, D. Perkins, L. Borden, & J. Keith (Eds.), *Community Youth Development: Programs, Policies, and Practices* (pp. 90–117). Sage Publications.

Suárez-Orozco, C., Gaytán, F. X., Bang, H. J., Pakes, J., O'Connor, E., & Rhodes, J. (2010). Academic trajectories of newcomer immigrant youth. *Developmental Psychology*, *46*(3), 602–618. https://psycnet.apa.org/doi/10.1037/a0018201

Questions to Consider

Invention

1. Assuming that Flemming was free to select her topic, how would you imagine she discovered her issue?

2. Imagine you were inspired by Flemming's causal analysis to examine the effects of motivation, participation, and assessment on a different group, such as new recruits in their first week of military boot camp. What would you do, and where would you look for information as you invent?

3. What information does Flemming appear to have discovered during research, and what did she develop or create herself?

Audience

4. The research Flemming found establishes a causal chain. How does she describe the relationships in this chain?

5. Why would a professor in an education psychology course ask students to write a cause-and-effect paper? What skills and competencies could such a paper demonstrate?

6. Flemming's voice is formal and direct. How do you think her voice would be different if she were to write an editorial arguing that public schools do not have the resources to support immigrant students?

Authority

7. Flemming is not a psychologist or educational expert. What does she do to make her findings and argument authoritative?

8. What types of evidence does she provide, and is the evidence sufficient to establish a cause-and-effect relationship?

9. What would you say is the major strength of Flemming's argument? How would you change her argument to make it more persuasive?

MODULE V-7

WHAT AUDIENCES EXPECT OF AN ANALYSIS AND EVALUATION

Although analysis and evaluation are two separate activities, and can be separate forms of writing, evaluation depends upon analysis, and analyses usually conclude with an assessment or evaluation of their subject.

- When you write an **analysis**, you examine a complex item, idea, or event by looking at its parts and considering how the parts work together.
- When you write an **evaluation**, you provide an assessment or judgment about the subject of your analysis. To make an assessment, you use standards of judgment, or **criteria**, to evaluate how the parts work together and comprise the larger item, idea, or event.

Genres such as movie reviews and customer reviews found on sites like Amazon and Yelp are all shaped by analysis and evaluation. As a student, you may be asked to analyze a work of literature and write a literary analysis. Or you may be asked to analyze a company's financial data and then evaluate its business plan. Professors of every discipline analyze and evaluate, and they will ask you to do the same. An analysis is sometimes all that is necessary for the assignment or writing situation, but in this chapter it is treated as an essential part of evaluation.

Why Would I Need to Analyze and Evaluate?

Three types of assignments or situations typically call for an analysis and evaluation: an assignment that asks you to explore an item, idea, or event; an assignment that requires you to demonstrate authority and competency; and an assignment that asks you to educate or inform an audience.

Exploring items, ideas, and events is what people who work at universities, research centers, intelligence agencies, and even some corporations do. Students are often asked to practice analysis and evaluation so that they can explore a subject on their own as opposed to simply being told what to think about it.

In a meteorology class, for example, you might be given a map that looks like a hairy United States and asked to do an analysis and evaluation to determine the best location for a wind turbine farm. The map in Figure 5.7 is an analysis of the speed and direction of prevailing winds on a given day. Using this analysis and a criterion, such as the wind speed necessary to generate 10 kilowatts of power, you could evaluate different possible locations and decide on the best place to locate a wind turbine.

Figure 5.7
United States
wind map.

Demonstrating authority and competency can be important for persuading your instructor that you have mastered your subject, which will in turn help you achieve a good grade. For example, in an engineering lab, you could be asked to explain why manhole covers are round and to prove your reasoning. To answer the question, you would need to conduct an analysis and evaluation by 1) analyzing round manhole covers, their purpose, and the purpose of the holes they cover; 2) developing criteria that you can use to see if other shapes might better meet these purposes; and 3) evaluating the other shapes to see if they meet your criteria. The question isn't really about your knowledge of manhole covers, though, but about your ability to analyze and evaluate solutions to problems as an engineer would.

Educating or informing an audience is another reason people analyze and evaluate subjects. Because this type of argument breaks complex subjects into parts and then examines the parts and how they work together, analysis and evaluation is also an excellent teaching tool. In an economics class, for example, a group assignment might call for your team to analyze the fuel burned per mile for a person traveling by plane and again by train. With this information, your team could then evaluate the carbon footprint, dollar cost, and other effects of both types of travel. For your class presentation, you would present your criteria, analysis, and evaluation so your audience can understand how you came to your findings. In this way, you would show your audience how an everyday decision can lead to costs of all kinds, both obvious and not-so-obvious.

A writer can shape an analysis and evaluation argument in many ways. However, an effective analysis and evaluation emerges from thoughtful invention and research, is attentive to the audience and their disposition, and has the authority not only to sound reasonable but also to have persuasive force.

Beginning Your Analysis with Invention and Research

Focus, scope, and discovery are the elements of an analysis and evaluation that set the direction of your analysis and keep you on track.

- **Focus:** The subject of your analysis is its focus. For example, a consumer review of the iPad mini focuses on the smaller version of Apple's popular iPad. A thoughtful invention process will help you identify and refine your focus.
- **Scope:** During the invention process, looking at other items, ideas, or events similar to your focus will help you analyze your subject. To analyze the iPad mini, for example, you would look at similar 7-inch electronic tablets. These tablets are your scope. If the members of your audience are thinking about buying a tablet, you would not include desktop computers in your analysis, but you might include larger tablets. If you decide to talk about an iPad in terms of a desktop, however, you'll need to make it clear to your audience why you chose such a large scope—with seemingly unrelated items—for your analysis.
- **Discovery:** In an analysis, the writer locates and names significant elements, traits, patterns, and strategies that make up the thing, idea, or event that is the focus. An analysis of the iPad mini's processor speed, battery life, and display quality will lead to specific data and findings you can use to compare it with the other tablets within your scope.

Shaping Your Analysis and Evaluation to Meet Audience Expectations

A chef looking at reviews of knives may be looking for durability and sharpness and may not care if a meat cleaver was forged at a foundry that uses renewable energy, just as someone reading a Yelp review of a farmer's market may be looking for one committed to the use of renewables and sustainable farming methods rather than a particular kind of vegetable or fruit. In other words, to write an effective, interesting analysis, you need a specific audience, and you need to know their disposition and expectations.

- **Criteria:** The criteria consist of the values, standards, or metrics you use to judge the evidence for your evaluation. The criteria you use to analyze and evaluate a subject should be shaped by
  - ◉ similar items, ideas, or events within your scope,
  - ◉ your purpose and your audience's expectations, and
  - ◉ the time and resources you have to analyze and evaluate.

Any item, idea, or event can be valued or measured in an astounding number of ways. For example, if the focus of your analysis and evaluation is Girl Scout Cookies, you could look at the energy used to produce a box of cookies. Or you could analyze and evaluate how the human body metabolizes a Thin Mint. As you can see, you have a great deal of creative freedom when deciding upon the criteria of your analysis and evaluation. Once you have determined your criteria, the evidence you will discover as you apply it will shape your argument.

In fact, your criteria will determine the evidence you use—and the evidence you exclude—in your argument. For example, if your criteria include measures such as tastiness, crispness, and sweetness, you will be arguing about the flavor and mouth feel of the cookies. If, however, your criteria are based on industrial baking practices, packaging technology, and shipping logistics, you will not be talking about the yummy goodness of Thin Mints. The argument you will be making with the latter criteria is based on the quality and efficiency of the industrial food-processing bakeries that hold the Girl Scout Cookie license.

When you are trying to narrow down the large number of possible values, standards, or metrics you could use to evaluate your subject, you must think of your purpose and the members of your audience, their expectations, needs, and disposition. Your audience may not care about the marketing of Girl Scout Cookies, only their flavor. An audience of marketing professionals, though, might feel differently. An evaluation of the iPad mini without a price comparison may not be of much use to a consumer. An app developer, on the other hand, may not care about price but needs an analysis and evaluation of the processor speed and memory capacity. If your purpose is to help parents select the best tablet for a seven-year-old, other metrics such as durability may be more important.

- **Evidence:** Your review of the criteria you used to analyze your subject will generate evidence for an evaluation. The analysis of the iPad mini, for example, provides evidence about its processor speed, display resolution, and battery life.

Making Your Assessment Persuasive by Establishing Authority

Your criteria may be composed of relevant metrics and your focus may be clear and relevant to your audience. However, for your readers to accept your analysis and evaluation, they must recognize your authority. And authority is determined by the reasoning and logic of your assessment. An assessment often describes the relationship between the subject analyzed and the broader scope into which it fits, and may look like this: "The iPad mini is best in its class of sub 8 inch tablets, and is a standout in terms of battery life. Its higher price, however, sets it apart from similar tablets." Or if you are writing an analysis of gourmet cookies for readers of a cooking and food magazine, and your criteria do not include flavor, your readers may question your reasoning. In addition, if the scope of your criteria is flavor and mouth feel, but your assessment focuses on packaging, a reader will have good reason to question how you came to your conclusions.

Genres that Analyze and Evaluate

The basic elements of an analysis and evaluation are always the same. However, each genre that analyzes and evaluates presents these elements differently. For example, a person's life history would be treated differently in a biography than it would be in a eulogy written for the family and friends attending a memorial service. The audience for a biography expects a detailed account of the subject's life and a dispassionate analysis and evaluation of their achievements, setbacks, and relationships. A eulogy may also analyze and evaluate, but it will commonly focus on positive personal qualities and achievements as recalled by those that loved and admired the deceased. Among the many genres that call for analysis and evaluation are the following:

- A **review of a cultural product such as a film, a streaming series, or a popular song** examines a specific work using qualities and traits found in similar, successful works of that genre. The reviewer then comments on the achievement of the work based on the criteria.
- **Image reviews** are used to identify common, innovative, and effective traits or qualities of images, as well as abnormalities and errors. A medical technician can evaluate an image to diagnose illnesses, for example.
- A **cost-benefit analysis** analyzes a plan or potential opportunity like a contract. The criteria are typically limited to financial or market-share metrics. Business and government groups use this genre of analysis to compare the impact of different business or policy options.
- A **literary analysis** considers the literary techniques that are evident within a poem or novel, for example, and evaluates how the techniques work to make a distinct, meaningful expression of the genre. Unlike a review, which indicates whether a book is worth reading, a literary analysis starts from the premise that the work is worthy of careful attention.

- A **product review** in a consumer publication is an application of criteria composed of practical metrics that are of concern to a consumer. A product review typically analyzes and evaluates a specific make or model of an item and then compares it to other makes and models, which are analyzed using the same criteria.

MODULE V-8

AN ANALYSIS AND EVALUATION GENRE: REVIEW OF A CULTURAL EVENT

Evaluations are common assignments in various college courses because they require you to think critically and evaluate a subject dispassionately, often using criteria or a method developed in a specific discipline such as analyzing the brush strokes of a Monet painting or the oxygen intake of an engine.

Alvaro Gonzalez wrote the following essay for an assignment in a college writing course. He had visited traditional museums on school field trips and was curious to see and write about an example of the "new museum movement" with an open design allowing for multiple interpretations of artifacts from different cultures. Also, he had never seen an exhibit focused solely on pre-Columbian people and cultures. As you read his essay, notice how his analysis informs his evaluation. Gonzalez also uses comparison and contrast in his evaluation of the success of the museum exhibit.

Jorge Pardo Brings the New Museum to LACMA
Alvaro Gonzalez

Surprisingly, the <u>world of museums</u> is a contentious battle-ground of ideas and visions. The struggle between the "New Museum" and the "Modern Museum" is one example of the war of ideas. *The new exhibit of the Los Angeles County Museum of Arts (LACMA) Pre-Columbian art collection* is an example of **a new, young curator attempting to advance New Museum ideals against dated Modern Museum expectations**.

The split between the New Museum movement and the more traditional Modern Museum plays out in many ways. In the new LACMA exhibit, the conflict between new and

Scope—world of museums

Focus—LACMA Pre-Columbian art exhibit

Assessment thesis —curator of exhibit trying something new

modern is most apparent in the *information provided, the architecture, and the museum/audience relationship.*

Criteria—information, architecture, museum/audience relationship

The Modern Museum rarely discloses the name of its curators or the ideals that inform their work. Because *Jorge Pardo, the curator of "Latin American Art: Ancient to Contemporary," and his vision for the exhibit were promoted with the opening of the collection*, the connection between the Art of the Americas exhibit and New Museum's ideologies is easily discoverable. *The architecture of the exhibit, which is very non-linear and immerses the audience, is the most obvious New Museum trait of the exhibit (Pardo).*

Evidence—curator identified, architecture flowing

The typical modern museum separates the audience and the gallery. The museum/audience relationship in the Modern museum model is cold and distant, as Eilean Hooper-Greenhill explains in *Museums and the Interpretation of Visual Culture* (7). It can be likened to the relationship between a boss behind a desk and an employee standing attentively, respectfully, and quietly in front of it. Pardo's

Discovery—museum ideal curator is working against

Fig. 1 One of the Latin American galleries at the Los Angeles County Museum of Art.

Evidence—non-traditional exhibition of artwork

exhibit calls for the same degree of attention and consideration, but it does so by breaking certain relational norms. *Pardo refuses to give into the structured norm of the modern boxed gallery museum. The pillars and the walls upon which the artworks are mounted are made of multi-layered, warm wood (fig. 1). In addition, the walls of the exhibit aren't white and straight but made of flowing curves, immersing the audience in a sense of motion. By giving the gallery motion, Pardo removes the idea that exhibits have a start and a finish line; he encourages free-range observing.*

Evidence of break with tradition—exhibit uses flowing wood

Jorge Pardo's exhibit attempts to build a closer bond between artifact and audience. Pardo draws his audience

Discovery—attempt to build closer bond

into the viewing experience without compromising or redefining everyday artifacts. An example of re-contextualization of the typical Modern Museum is seen in the Lando Hall of California History where **baskets and tools are placed next to a recreated hut behind glass.** This approach separates the audience from the artifacts, often losing the genuine artifact in the larger and possibly inaccurate recreation.

Discovery—artifacts traditionally exhibited

The majority of the pieces of the Pre-Columbian art exhibit are items for everyday use such as vessels for grain or for drinking, spoons and forks, items used for sport, and even dolls.

Discovery—artifacts of new exhibit

Pardo's exhibit encourages the appreciation of the intrinsic qualities and details of the artifacts by placing them in the traffic flow. He varies the sight lines and uses juxtaposition. At one point Pardo asks us to reconsider contemporary art by placing modern lounge furnishings within a Pre-Columbian cave.

Evidence—new exhibit highlights intrinsic qualities

One element of the Pardo exhibit grates against the New Museum approach. **The anthropological wallpaper identifying artifacts with the times of their creation, created by Pardo, encourages passive observation instead of an active learner experience.** This effect detracts greatly from the overall exhibit.

Assessment—wallpaper does not fit New Museum ideals

The museum and Pardo as curator have attempted to distinguish this most recent LACMA exhibit by breaking many established Modernist ideals. **Pardo does a good job of breaking away from the established traditions of the Modern Museum and creates a more captivating exhibit that aligns itself with new ways of imagining the museum.** Though there are shortcomings, such as the anthropological wallpaper, Pardo demonstrates what is possible when we break away from the Modern museum. Not only can the presentation of the artifacts change, the entire exhibit can be transformed.

Assessment—exhibit an immersive break from tradition

Works Cited

Hooper-Greenhill, Eilean. "Culture and Meaning in the Museum." *Museums and the Interpretation of Visual Culture*, Routledge, 2000, pp. 127–30.

Pardo, Jorge. "Latin American Art: Ancient to Contemporary." Los Angeles County Museum of Art, 27 July 2008.

MLA citations

Questions to Consider

Invention

1. Gonzalez could have written about any museum exhibit in his city. What do you think prompted him to write about this subject?
2. How do you think Gonzalez gathered ideas, information, and evidence for his argument?
3. What did he discover about his subject?
4. What evidence tells you that the Gonzalez's essay is an analysis and evaluation?

Audience

5. What restrictions or limits did Gonzalez place on himself, and what expectations do you think he was responding to?
6. How does Gonzalez's essay differ from other types of academic writing like a research paper?
7. Who is Gonzalez writing to, and how do you know?

Authority

8. How does Gonzalez let the reader know that what he has discovered and what he says about his subjects can be trusted?
9. What has Gonzalez left out, and why do you think he did so?
10. How successful is Gonzalez's review? What could he do to make his essay stronger and more persuasive?

MODULE V-9

WHAT AUDIENCES EXPECT OF A PROPOSAL

A **proposal argument** is intended to persuade an audience to accept a solution to a problem or undertake a specific response to an opportunity. To do that, it identifies and informs the audience of a problem or opportunity, proposes a solution or response, shows with evidence and reasoning that the solution or response is superior to or more beneficial than other solutions or responses, and assures the audience that the solution will solve the problem or the response will achieve the stated goal.

Why Would I Need to Write a Proposal?

If you want to start a dance crew, change a zoning law, sell your bike on Craigslist, negotiate a labor contract, or propose marriage, you need to explain how things will be better in the future if your audience accepts your proposal today. In fact, if you want to bring about any change that you cannot do alone, a well-crafted proposal is the way to move others to help you achieve your ambition, campaign, agreement, or vision.

In academic settings, professors often assign proposals to develop specific competencies and writing skills such as "create a marketing strategy," "apply for a research grant," or "offer an alternative reading of a novel or data set." Professors also use proposal assignments to assess the ability of students to apply what they have learned. For example, in a political science class, your professor may ask you to study a number of Senate election campaigns and then propose a campaign strategy for an imaginary candidate. In a course with a service learning or applied learning project, you may be asked to develop a proposal that identifies a local problem and proposes a solution.

Types of Proposals: Practical and Policy Proposals

One way to think about proposal arguments is to examine their focus and scope. If a proposal deals with an immediate, practical problem, such as the need for a new labor contract or to replace your old bike, then it is a **practical proposal**. The scope of a practical proposal is limited to whatever is needed to respond to the problem or opportunity. The focus is on the specifics of the problem or opportunity, the specifics of the fix or response, and details such as when the solution should be in place and how the opportunity will work.

On the other hand, a **policy proposal** is focused on larger, more general issues and has a larger scope. Most of the people who joined the fight for net neutrality—the idea that Internet service providers should treat all content equally and not favor or block particular content or websites—probably stated their position but did not suggest detailed regulations for the Federal Communications Commission to enforce. Rather, they focused on preserving the general policy of net neutrality.

The reasoning and evidence supporting practical proposals are different from those supporting policy proposals. The memos proposing a Galactic Network drafted by J.C.R. Licklider described general benefits and not the specifics of how such a network would work. But once the Advanced Research Projects Agency (ARPA) was on board, practical proposals followed, including solutions to real networking challenges, detailed schematics, and designs of switches and routers.

No matter what type of proposal you are writing, you might think of it as a way of helping your audience overcome a series of obstacles. Overcoming obstacles requires preparation, an understanding of the obstacles ahead, and an understanding of your team's capacities. When it comes to building an effective proposal, invention is your preparation.

Using Invention to Develop a Proposal

When using invention to develop a proposal, always consider the following two elements:

1. **A problem or opportunity**: Before your audience can decide to adopt your proposal, they must be aware of the problem or opportunity. Next, they must understand that it is a serious problem they can help to solve or a significant opportunity they can seize.

   For example, if you try to persuade your readers to support Title II reclassification of ISPs under the Communications Act of 1934, you are unlikely to inspire much excitement in your audience. However, with some thoughtful invention and careful research, you can recast your proposal in terms your audience will grasp: the Internet will slow down if you do not add your voice to the campaign for net neutrality.

2. **A solution**: Once your audience members recognize that the problem or opportunity you describe is important and urgent, they will expect a solution or a way to respond. Research will help you discover how others have responded to similar problems or opportunities as well as how previous proposals have failed or been ignored.

   In 2008, a young man surprised his girlfriend with a marriage proposal during a Houston Rockets basketball game. He was rejected at center court and left holding the ring box. Clutch, the Rockets mascot walked him off the court. Clearly, the proposal made perfect sense in his head, but it is just as clear that he did not do his research or fully think through all the possibilities. Research your audience so your proposal has a chance.

Making Your Proposal Acceptable to Your Audience

Thinking about the following aspects of a proposal will help you tailor it to your audience:

- **A Focus on the Right Audience**: It may seem obvious to say that proposals should be made only to those who might adopt your solution, but proposals are often made to the wrong audience.

  For example, you may be able to persuade North American college students to accept your proposal for new laws ending government censorship of the Internet in China. However, they have no power to bring about such a change.

The only individuals who could act on such a proposal are members of the Chinese Communist Party. In fact, the US government, as well as companies like Google and Facebook, have repeatedly proposed to the Chinese Foreign Ministry that they should tear down the "Great Firewall," arguing that such censorship harms trade relations.

- **A Rational, Doable, and Effective Call to Action**: Part of the challenge of building a persuasive proposal is rising above the noise of the countless proposals, opportunities, advertisements, and solutions we hear every day. To stand out, you must show that your solution or response is superior to earlier or competing proposals. A rational, doable, and effective call to action is more likely to be heard.

  The Battle for the Net consortium, a group of technology companies and nonprofit advocacy organizations, had only five days to pressure the FCC to adopt net-neutrality regulations (see http://blog.cloudflare.com/battleforthenet/). To rise above the noise, participating websites had to show that their proposal was more widely supported than those opposed to the regulations. The consortium also had to overcome apathy and motivate as many comments as possible. With three easy clicks of a mouse, anyone on the Internet could overcome seemingly large obstacles, a large government bureaucracy influenced by powerful lobbyists, and act. The campaign demonstrates that the persuasive power of a proposal is based not only on the reasoning and evidence but also on the audience's understanding of why and how to take action.

- **Incentives**: "Change is hard" may be one of the only clichés that is as overused as it is true. You want your readers to believe, think, or behave differently, but it is usually so much easier for them to continue as they have done in the past. And how they have thought about and done things in the past has worked out pretty well. When developing your proposal, keep in mind that you must offer real incentives that motivate your audience in three ways:
  - the future benefits of adopting the proposal overwhelm the audience's natural instinct to resist change;
  - change is easier than simply ignoring the proposal and worth the effort given the proposed benefits; and
  - urgent action is necessary to ensure the proposed benefits.

Making Your Proposal Authoritative

To convince an audience to adopt it, a successful proposal has the following elements:

- **Reasons and evidence**: Before your audience will act upon a solution or response, they must believe that a problem or opportunity is real and that the solution or response is rational and doable. By offering compelling reasons and solid evidence to back them up, you can convince your audience to believe you and adopt your proposal. In other words, reasons and evidence establish your authority.

Your reasoning does not have to be sophisticated, but it must resonate with your intended audience. When Emma Watson addressed the United Nations to promote the "HeForShe" Campaign, her intended audience was men and boys who were put off by the word "feminist." Watson proposed that the word itself was not important, but rather that gender inequality and gender stereotypes are serious problems that also affect men. She argued that too many young men silently suffer mental illness for fear of being considered less of a man if they ask for help. To prove her point, she cited statistics from a report entitled "Suicides in the United Kingdom, 2013 Registrations," proving that young British men are more likely to die by suicide than from auto accidents, cancer, and heart disease. She concluded that more young men are likely to die of suicide if the current trend is not reversed. In this way, she recast what some men and boys see as a feminist issue into a shared experience that inhibits and injures all generations.

- **Alternative solutions and conviction about the best solution**: You must convince your reader or listener that your proposed solution is the best possible one. Therefore, you must present alternatives, analyze each fairly, and then explain why they will not provide the desired result. Once you have eliminated alternative solutions and responses, your audience will look to you for a better option that will solve the problem or a better response that will result in the opportunity described. Conviction happens in the minds of your audience members, so you must build it for them.

  For example, if your history-major roommate proposed to build and host your website for a dollar a month, it is unlikely that you would (or should) simply accept the offer. However, if your roommate has provided an impressive portfolio of websites she built and maintains, along with a stack of thank-you notes and letters from happy customers, you might do well to hire her.

- **Integrity**: How your audience responds to your proposal may depend upon whether you are presenting a **transparent argument** so the audience can understand your purpose. If your audience can see that your proposal is not motivated simply by self-interest, that their future and yours will both be better if your proposal is adopted, they are more likely to be persuaded. On the other hand, if your purpose remains obscure, your audience will be suspicious. And as you know, suspicion does not lead to persuasion. But integrity is persuasive.

  For example, imagine you see what would normally be a $500 bike for sale on Craigslist for $300, and the seller will meet only at a Best Buy parking lot. You would be right to be suspicious. However, if the seller also has stated that she is leaving for the Peace Corps in a week and she wants to meet where she works for security reasons, you understand that her purpose is reasonable. Transparent arguments are persuasive because they contribute to your authority.

Genres that Propose a Solution

Proposals are a part of everyday life, and people have been composing proposals for as long as they have found reasons to work together. Tradition provides several genres of proposals that have proven effective in very different situations:

- **Position paper**: a written statement of an individual's or organization's views, disposition, or response toward an issue, policy, or question. It often includes counter-positions or counter-proposals.
- **Pop-up advertisement**: an online advertisement designed to entice or draw viewers to another website providing goods and services.
- **Advocacy speech**: a speech made on behalf of, and for the benefit of, an individual or a group, or a speech in support of a position or proposal.
- **Op-ed piece**: a brief persuasive argument typically found in a magazine, newspaper, or news site ("opposite the editorial") in which the author proposes a way of thinking, believing, or acting.
- **Proposed budget**: a financial estimate of future costs, obligations, and expenses.
- **Business proposal**: a text written to describe a business transaction to a potential client or customer. The proposal includes the goods and services offered, anticipated outcomes, and the price of the goods or services.

MODULE V-10

A PROPOSAL GENRE: POSITION PAPER

Veronica Pacheco wrote the following position paper as part of her "College Composition" portfolio. This context implies that the professor is the audience. However, the way in which Pacheco describes the problem of endangered sharks suggests that she has another intended audience in mind as well, namely those who care about animals or the environment but are unaware of the practice and impact of shark finning.

Consider the Shark
Veronica Pacheco

Although sharks in movies like *Sharknado* and *Jaws* are portrayed as cold, vicious killers, sharks are like other animals; they can feel pain. *Shark finning, on the other hand is cold and vicious. It is the practice of slicing off a shark's fins while the shark is still alive and throwing it back into the ocean* ("Shark Education"). *Shark fins are harvested for the sake of a single kind of soup. The Chinese are the largest consumers of shark fin soup, a delicacy at banquets and important dinners. For the sake of this soup, 99% of shark protein is wasted, these animals are put through unnecessary suffering, and shark finning threatens the balance of the oceans' ecosystems.*

Sharks should no longer be hunted solely for their fins because the methods are inhumane, finning threatens the ecosystem, and there are alternatives that will protect the wild population.

Shark finning is cruel and inhumane and must end. After a shark is caught and the fins sliced off, the live shark is tossed back into the water. Unable to swim, the shark slowly sinks toward the bottom where it is defenseless and can take days to die an agonizing death as it is eaten alive by other fish ("Shark Education"). Finning is inhumane. In addition, some of the methods used to catch sharks are harmful to the environment. Longline fishing practices are the most significant cause of losses in shark populations worldwide. Longlining involves floating a main line, around 100 feet, on the surface of the water while smaller secondary lines are baited and hang beneath the main line. Longline fishing is indiscriminate; all kinds of sharks are attracted to the bait. Experts estimate that within a decade most species of sharks will be lost because of longlining ("Longline Fishing").

Currently, twenty species of sharks are listed as endangered by the International Union for Conservation of Nature (IUCN). Since 1972, populations of many shark species have fallen by over 90% ("Shark Education"). As the graph below shows (fig. 1), shark populations have collapsed in the Northwest Atlantic where the US longline fishing fleet is based. Through careful management, though, a few species are making a comeback.

Margin annotations:

Problem: shark finning

Thesis: stop animal cruelty and protect the ecosystem

Reason: finning causes unreasonable and unnecessary suffering

Reason: longline fishing kills many species indiscriminately

Reason: many species of sharks are endangered

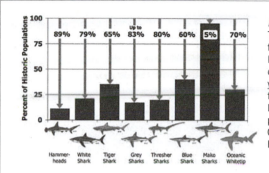

Fig. 1
The research team led by Julia Baum collected data from 15 years of longline fishing trawler logbooks. Graph provided by Tobey Curtis and the Fisheries Blog.

Loss and devastation of shark populations around the world affects the oceans and those who depend on shark meat as a main food source in third world countries. If longlining and shark finning continue to increase, these practices will inevitably lead to the extinction of shark species. Hence, the oceanic ecosystems of the world will forever be altered.

Why bother saving the sharks? Sharks and humans alike are both part of the food web. Every organism depends on other species and the ecosystem as a whole to survive. The extinction of sharks impacts not only the sharks but also all the other organisms such as small fish. A reduction in sharks can lead to a reduction in seafood that serves as a source of nutrition for a large segment of the world's population. For example, tiger sharks are key to the quality of seagrass beds and ecosystem balance. If that shark population is greatly reduced, then the ray population will explode, causing a significant drop in medium sized fish and green sea turtles, which live and feed in seagrass beds ("Shark Education"). Without tiger sharks to control their prey's foraging, this important habitat will be lost. **The balance of biodiversity is vital to life.**

How do we start to fix this problem? **Breeding sharks specifically for culinary purposes in shark farms would enable humane harvesting methods and leave the wild shark population untouched.** Finning is illegal in federal waters; however, enforcement on the ocean is nearly impossible ("Shark Education"). Because shark farms could be regulated, raising sharks for food could be made as humane as possible.

Another solution would be to change the appetites of those who buy and consume shark fins. **A number of organizations**

Reason: reduced shark population affects ocean and people

Incentive: protect biodiversity, which protects seafood stock

Solution: shark farms

have held contests asking renowned chefs to develop soup recipes without fins, and the results are encouraging.

Further, a change in the overall attitudes about sharks can make a difference. Let's face it, sharks are unappealing, unlike cute polar bear cubs and other endangered species. However, **Shark Week on the Discovery Channel has already done a great deal to help people understand and respect these complex creatures.** Clearly, television programs alone won't save sharks from suffering painful, wasteful deaths. However, as Shark Week shows, the negative connotation that surrounds sharks can be changed, and further efforts will continue to make people more inclined to contribute to the cause.

Clearly, shark finning is an inhumane fishing method and the ways the fins are harvested are wasteful and cruel. **You may not eat shark fin soup, but you can protect sharks by boycotting and protesting restaurants that serve such soup. Share the story of sharks and the inhumane act of finning, and join and support international organizations that are dedicated to protecting the shark and marine ecosystems, such as Sea Shepherd, the Humane Society International, and Wild Aid.** *These organizations are having an impact,* **and by joining them you can ensure that they continue to work to protect sharks.** The next time you hear the daunting theme music from the movie *Jaws*, instead of screaming in fear, just consider the shark.

> Solution: change appetites

> Solution: change attitudes

> Conviction: attitudes are changing

Works Cited

Baum, Julia K., et al. "Collapse and Conservation of Shark Populations in the Northwest Atlantic." *Science*, vol. 299, no. 5605, 2003, pp. 389–92. www.jstor.org/stable/3833388.

Curtis, Tobey. "Jaws Returns: Signs of Recovery in Well-Managed Shark Populations." *The Fisheries Blog*, 4 June 2012, the fisheriesblog.com/2012/06/04/jaws-returns-signs-of-recovery-in-well-managed-shark-populations/.

"Longline Fishing Threatens Seabirds and Other Marine Life." *The Humane Society of the United States*, 25 Sept. 2009, www.humanesociety.org/issues/fisheries/facts/longline_fishing_marine_life.html.

"Shark Education—Shark Finning Facts." *Sharkwater*, Sharkwater Productions, 2016, www.sharkwater.com/index.php/shark-education/. Accessed 12 Oct. 2016.

> MLA format

Questions to Consider

Invention

1. A proposal is often an answer to a question. What question do you imagine Pacheco was trying to answer with her proposal?
2. Where do you think Pacheco looked for her initial research about her subject and audience?
3. What information and data appear to be discoveries Pacheco made during research?

Audience

4. Based on her language and examples, what can you infer about the audience that Pacheco had in mind for her proposal?
5. What resistance would Pacheco's proposal have to overcome in the minds of its intended readers?

Authority

6. How does Pacheco build conviction that her proposal is possible and doable and will have the desired effects?
7. Pacheco is not an expert on the subject she writes or speaks about here. What does she do to establish authority?
8. Pacheco wrote this proposal in response to a class assignment. How would her attempt to establish authority be different if she were writing an op-ed for a local newspaper?

CHAPTER 6
POLISHING ARGUMENTS

LOGICAL FALLACIES DEFINED

A **logical fallacy** is an error or breakdown in an argument's reasoning. One way to classify logical fallacies is by the type of logic that breaks down:

- A **formal fallacy** is a breakdown in the structure and reasoning of a deductive argument.
- An **informal fallacy**, on the other hand, is caused by a breakdown in the meaning, language, and expression of an inductive argument.

Because inductive arguments do not depend upon a rigid form, they can fail, mislead, confuse, or deceive in many different ways. The logical fallacies that follow are all informal fallacies. Module I-1 describes deductive and inductive reasoning.

Misleading Readers: Fallacies of Relevance

When an argument wanders away from its original subject, it leads the audience away from the central claim or to a conclusion that is not supported by the evidence. Fallacies of relevance can happen when writers are careless or make mistakes of scope and focus. They can also be intentional. Here is a list of the most common fallacies of relevance.

1. Appeal to false authority

You would be lucky to get acting advice from a star like Gwyneth Paltrow. However, she is not an authority on menopause or vitamin and supplement protocols such as the "Goop Wellness Madame Ovary" that her company Goop sells and she promotes as providing "support for thyroid health as well as things like mild hot flashes, mood shifts, and stress-related fatigue." Audiences fall for the **appeal to false authority** fallacy if they are distracted by the fame or impressive-sounding title of the person being cited. If someone claims that an authority or expert supports her or his argument, check the expert's credentials and note whether he or she actually is a recognized expert on the subject of the argument.

Figure 6.1
Gwyneth Paltrow is the founder and CEO of Goop, a lifestyle company.

2. Appeal to ignorance

An **appeal to ignorance** states that a position must be correct because no one has proven it wrong. Someone who uses this fallacy distracts the audience by pointing out a lack of contrary evidence. For example, if someone were to argue that the bright spots on the dwarf planet Ceres, discovered by the Dawn spacecraft in 2015, are probably examples of alien technology because no one has proven otherwise, the argument would be a fallacy. A lack of contrary evidence does not mean that aliens are on Ceres or predict what evidence yet to be discovered will prove. Audiences that accept the true vs. false thinking do not consider other possible explanations that may be discovered in the future.

3. Appeal to fear

A person whose argument tries to make you afraid of the people holding opposing views, or tries to prejudice you against an alternative position by making you fear what will happen if you do not agree with a claim, is using an **appeal to fear**. For example, people wanting to gain your support for blocking the arrival of immigrants from a specific part of the world might say that if we let those immigrants in there will be terrorist attacks in America, just like those in Europe. Terrorism is a serious concern, but stoking fears of violence and then linking that fear to an entire group is simply unjust and irrational. An audience persuaded by fear is convinced only as long as the fear remains, because real conviction comes from critical thinking, reasoning, and evidence.

4. Appeal to tradition

A person who ignores your proposal for change by saying we have always done it this way is using an **appeal to tradition**, diverting attention from the merits of your proposal to look instead at the past or at a tradition. For example, when grandpa says, it is tradition that the eldest son takes over the family business, he is not considering the talents and preferences of the eldest son or of others in the family. What was or has been may have merits. However, simply pointing to tradition is not an argument based on the merits of tradition, nor is it a rational evaluation of an alternative way of doing things.

5. Bandwagon fallacy

The pressure of **groupthink**, the tendency of people to agree with other members of their group, makes the **bandwagon fallacy** difficult to recognize and hard to resist, especially if the group consists of your friends or a crowd you want to be a part of. For example, if your friends say "everyone will think you're lame if you don't do shots with us," they are not making a claim for the benefits of shots. They are simply applying pressure. Audience members fall for this fallacy if they base the truth or value of an argument on the number of people who accept it or on a fear of being left out (Figure 6.2).

Figure 6.2
The bandwagon fallacy.

6. Personal attack or *ad hominem*

If someone disagrees with your argument by calling you names, criticizing your appearance, or attacking other personal qualities, that person is leading you and the audience away from the subject—your argument—by using an *ad hominem fallacy*. For example, when someone running for office says that his opponent isn't ready to lead because, after all, he has had only one job his entire life, and that's as a farmer, the speaker is distracting the audience from important issues such as the candidate's qualifications and policies. If you or an audience responds to such an attack by denying the insults, being defensive, or hollering names back, you have fallen for this fallacy.

7. Faulty analogy

An **analogy** links two subjects to make a statement about a common relationship or shared qualities and characteristics. For example, comparing how the brain stores information to how a computer stores data can be helpful. However, a **faulty analogy** draws attention away from the subject of an argument to a thing, idea, or event that is not comparable. For example, the claim that a brain retains memory the way a sponge holds water is a faulty analogy: water is a substance held in a sponge's cells by surface tension, while a memory is information encoded as electrical impulses and stored in the mind's neural net. An audience is distracted by a faulty analogy when they accept the mischaracterization of a thing, idea, or event.

Confusing Readers: Fallacies of Ambiguity

A vague, poorly worded, or disorganized argument can lead the audience to accept conclusions that have not been proven or supported by the evidence. Fallacies of ambiguity may be intentional, but they are more often caused by a failure to consider how the audience will understand the words, sentences, and organization of an argument. Though such mistakes often merely confuse readers or listeners, the following fallacies can also lead to false conclusions.

8. Equivocation fallacy

Words are slippery because most of them have multiple meanings. Speakers use the **equivocation fallacy** when they use two different meanings of a word in their argument. For example, the following is an equivocation fallacy: "Yes, a liberal arts college is an option, but I want my daughter to see both sides of politics and not just learn liberal ideas." "Liberal" in the phrase "liberal arts" means a broad range of subjects suited to a free society. However, the speaker shifts the meaning of the word "liberal" to mean a political ideology sometimes contrary to conservative ideas. An audience that does not notice the shift in meaning or accepts it is duped by an equivocation fallacy.

9. Straw man

A person who falsely claims that you hold a dubious position on an issue and then easily disproves the position is using a **straw man fallacy** to confuse the audience. In the following example, the straw man appears when the speaker summarizes the opposing argument: "My opponent says he wants to give illegal immigrants, who are all lawbreakers, a path to citizenship. In essence, he wants to let criminals go free and only enforce the laws he likes. But we don't have a choice. We can't let criminals walk free." The claim that serious crimes should be prosecuted is an easy debate to win, which is why this argument is set up as a straw man so that it can be easily knocked down. The actual immigration debate is far more complex, however. Just as it is easier to knock down a straw-filled scarecrow than a real person, an audience that falls for this fallacy mistakes the weak argument for the opposition's real argument.

Deceiving Readers: Fallacies of Presumption

A **presumption** is a belief that is not supported by evidence. If a presumption informs or is part of an argument yet remains unseen or unstated, it can result in a deceptive conclusion that appears true but has no real support in reason or evidence.

10. Begging the question/circular reasoning

Begging the question begins where it ends. The **begging the question fallacy** assumes the conclusion is true and uses the conclusion as evidence to support the argument. In a valid argument, reasoning links claims that are supported by evidence to a logical conclusion (Figure 6.3).

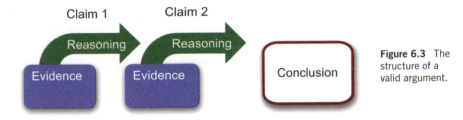

Figure 6.3 The structure of a valid argument.

In an argument that begs the question, however, the conclusion circles back to replace evidence or a claim, leading to a circular argument (Figure 6.4).

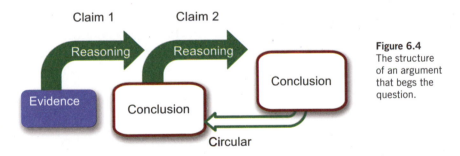

Figure 6.4 The structure of an argument that begs the question.

An argument that begs the question sounds like this: "Candidate X was a great governor and is the best presidential candidate because all the other candidates are inferior." An audience may not recognize circular reasoning if the conclusion is rephrased when it is used as evidence, as in the example above.

11. False dilemma/either-or fallacy

In a debate, if your opponent tries to force you to choose between only two options, she has placed you in a **false dilemma**, sometimes called the **either-or fallacy**. For example, the argument that either we send all the illegal immigrants back or we grant them all amnesty reduces a complex issue with many possible responses to an either-or decision. The deception here is that there are actually more than two responses to the issue of illegal or undocumented immigration. If audience members resist this fallacy by failing to choose between the two options, they can be portrayed as avoiding the problem or being indecisive.

12. Hasty generalization fallacy

Suppose a friend mentioned to you that Nebraskans always wear red, claiming she knows this because she walked down O Street on Saturday and every person she saw was wearing something red. It is true that red is a popular color in Nebraska, but a different sample of Nebraskans on a different day would prove that the closets in Nebraska hold a rainbow of colors. Audiences fall for the **hasty generalization fallacy** when they are directed away from considering additional observations, or accept a small sample size (Nebraskans on O Street in Lincoln on football Saturday) as large enough—and representative enough—to make a more general statement.

13. *Post hoc ergo propter hoc* fallacy

It's often tempting to conclude that one event caused another because the first event immediately preceded the second one. This reasoning—known as *post hoc, ergo propter hoc* or "after this, therefore, because of this"—is a fallacy. Closeness in time, or correlation, does not by itself prove that a cause-effect relationship exists between the two events. For example, imagine you said the following to your sister: "It seems that since you started cheering for the Crunch, they haven't won a soccer game. Before you became a fan, they were in the running for the MASL championship. Clearly, you are bad luck." Your belief that your sister caused the slump is fallacious. You can watch out for this fallacy in your own arguments or those of others by considering other possible causes or simply by refusing to accept a causal claim without evidence.

14. Slippery slope/camel's nose fallacy

A **slippery slope fallacy**, also called a **camel's nose fallacy**, suggests that one thing will inevitably lead to another. For example, if you slip on a slope, you will slide all the way to the bottom. Or if you let a camel stick its nose inside your tent, soon the whole animal will be sitting inside. Or a professor may say that if she allows you to hand in your paper late, soon everyone in class will be late with their papers. People who use this fallacy are trying to persuade you to accept a chain of events leading to an undesirable consequence, without offering evidence that these events will actually happen. Valid cause-effect arguments provide evidence for each causal relationship in a chain and acknowledge alternative causes and other possible effects. See Module V-5 for more on causal arguments.

15. Sweeping generalization fallacy

When people apply a general rule to all situations, they are making a **sweeping generalization**. For example, people who say that everyone must avoid sugar are speaking too broadly, because the best way to treat sudden hypoglycemia is to eat raw sugar or a candy bar. A person who passes out because of low blood sugar is an exception, of course, but just such an exception proves that you cannot sweep all situations under a single general rule. An audience may fall for this fallacy if an argument hides exceptions or neglects to consider them (Figure 6.5).

Figure 6.5
Mother Chicken's statement may make sense, but it is a sweeping generalization.

Logical fallacies occur because they are part of everyday thinking and grow out of common activities like making sense of the world and protecting ourselves or those we love. Or they are simply the result of human error. However, if we consciously choose to use logical fallacies in our writing and public arguments, or decide not to fix the accidental fallacies we discover, we are no longer making a common error. Instead, we are making a moral decision.

Speakers or writers who deliberately use fallacies are choosing to mislead, confuse, or deceive their audience. That kind of choice will affect how others see them and how they can or are allowed to engage the world. In short, people are known by their words, and authority in academic settings is based upon honest and valid reasoning.

It is true that some public figures and writers are intentionally provocative and use fallacies all the time with little negative effect. Then again, such figures and writers are typically preaching to the choir: their supporters have no reason to check the logic of arguments they agree with. In an academic setting, you will typically be making arguments to people who don't agree with you but may do so if you are well reasoned and authoritative. Again, it comes down to a choice. How do you want to be known, and what do you want to be able to do?

Types of Appeals in Logical Fallacies

Logical fallacies can also be categorized by the type of appeals (*pathos*, *ethos*, and *logos*) that characterizes them. For example, a hasty generalization such as a survey of 20 college students indicates that most college students are unhappy with their major sounds like it is based on evidence and solid reasoning, or a *logos* appeal. Below you will find the most common fallacies organized by appeal type.

Pathos Appeals	Example
Appeal to False Authority	Champion soccer player Kathy Johnson recommends Vitafresh granola bars.
Appeal to Ignorance	No one has complained about Professor Snape, so he must be a good teacher.
Appeal to Tradition	My grandparents, parents, and siblings were all business majors, so I can't major in English.
Personal Attack / *Ad hominem*	My opponent is just a lonely, frustrated woman. That's why she's advocating ending the football program at our high school.
Straw Man	My opponent says we must enforce immigration laws. He wants to rip families apart, but that is not who we are.

Logos Appeals	Example
Faulty Analogy	Taking my ear buds without asking me is like what the big banks did to the economy in 2008.
Equivocation Fallacy	Being kind is the right thing to do, which is why I have a right to be treated with kindness.
Begging the Question / Circular Reasoning	Clearly, the first ranked Bulldog football team is the best in the nation—just look at the polls.
Hasty Generalization Fallacy	These two apples are bad; better throw out the whole barrel of apples.
Post hoc ergo propter hoc Fallacy	Every time I wear my blue suit I get bumped to first class. Clearly the gate agents appreciate fine tailoring.
Slippery Slope / Camel's Nose Fallacy	If you skip a workout today, it will be easier to skip a workout next week. Then you will just give up and never work out again.
Sweeping Generalization Fallacy	Fifty percent of people who start a Ph.D. program drop out, so I am not going to grad school because I want a better than 50 / 50 chance of success.

Ethos Appeals	Example
Bandwagon Fallacy	Everyone is voting for Katherine. If you don't what does that say about you?
Appeal to Fear	We don't know who is entering our country, but we do know terrorists want to hurt us.
False Dilemma / Either-Or Fallacy	It's simple: either you support the Patriot Act or you let the terrorists win.

MODULE VI-2

AWKWARDNESS AND FLOW DEFINED

If you were asked to name the smoothest dancer or athlete you have ever seen, you might think of someone like the ballet dancer Misty Copeland or the basketball star Stephen Curry. You recognize brilliant dancers or basketball players by the flow and accuracy of their movements. But if you had to teach your cousin, who moves like a baby giraffe on ice, how to dance like Copeland or drive like Curry, you might be at a loss.

You know smoothness, elegant movement, and flow when you see them, and you can detect awkwardness just as easily. But trying to define which moves are smooth and which are awkward is difficult. In fact, no movement of a leg or hand is inherently awkward or smooth. Your perception of them depends on the situation. If you were to put Curry on a dance floor or Copeland on a basketball court, their physical talents would probably still be apparent, but they would seem out of place and wrong.

What is true on the dance floor or the basketball court is also true of writing: the audience and their expectations shape how a sentence is perceived. An awkward sentence isn't simply a mishmash of jittery punctuation, sloppy subject-verb agreement, or confusing sentence structure, though such things can lead to a breakdown in flow. Instead, readers experience jitteriness and confusion when they read a sentence that is structured in an unexpected way, given the situation.

For example, read the following opening sentence to *Signatures of the Visible*, written by Fredric Jameson, a renowned, award-winning professor of comparative literature. How do you experience this passage as you read?

> The visual is essentially pornographic, which is to say that it has its end in rapt, mindless fascination; thinking about its attributes becomes an adjunct to that, if it is unwilling to betray its object; while the most austere films necessarily draw their energy from the attempt to repress their own excess (rather than from the more thankless effort to discipline the viewer).

Readers who are unfamiliar with Jameson's writing are likely to be disturbed by the style and abstract reasoning in this passage. However, readers who know Jameson's work recognize the excerpt above as an example of his "dialectical prose"—a style of writing that forces the reader to experience the contradictions and discontinuities that Jameson finds in the texts and images he critiques. Not only does Jameson's intended audience expect his convoluted sentences and ambiguity, but readers who seek out Jameson's writing may also find his very long, complicated sentences and reasoning to be as elegant as chaînés executed by Misty Copeland.

On the other hand, imagine you were asked to write a review of *Signatures of the Visible* for the campus newspaper. Your readers would expect clear writing with standard sentences and specific words and phrases that avoid unnecessary abstractness. Unfair? Not exactly.

Jameson's intentionally awkward constructions and reasoning mean that his book is accessible to a very small, specialized audience: Marxist literary critics or scholars of postmodernism. When you write using easily accessible sentences and phrases, a large, broad audience can understand your argument and potentially be persuaded by your reasoning.

Written work is considered **awkward** when it is difficult for readers to process and frustrates their ability to perceive meaning. Think of awkwardness as speed bumps, your writing as a road, and your reader as a driver. Any time drivers have to slow down for a speed bump, they will become frustrated.

For most readers, including professors reading student work, spelling errors, grammar errors, and sentences that are too short or too long are awkward speed bumps. In addition, words or phrases that the reader does not know can bring that reader to a dead stop.

The opposite of a bumpy road is a highway that flows. When writing **flows** it is easy for readers to understand, and they can effortlessly follow the development of an idea in a paragraph or passage. Writers achieve flow when they understand what the audience expects in a sentence, paragraph, or longer piece of writing. Writers can also achieve flow by appealing to readers' unconscious preferences or by using tricks of the trade that make reading easier. For example, alternating sentence length and using graphics effectively can result in a sense of flow.

Awkward writing has these common causes:

- Staying in your head, or not getting peer reviews or other opinions about your writing, when you are composing a public argument.
- Not knowing or not considering your audience members' perspective, thoughts, or knowledge.
- Not revising and not proofreading, or ignoring the traits and qualities your audience looks for in authoritative texts and voices.

During the invention stage, first and early drafts will always seem awkward to others, because they are your unpolished thoughts and ideas. However, a thoughtful invention stage will set you up well for the revision stage. Necessarily, the revision stage of your writing process is the crucial step in crafting your private thoughts for public consideration. The revision and proofreading stages are also where you craft your authoritative voice and style.

Flow Checklist

The following checklist will help you work with awkward sentences to create an experience of flow for your audience.

- Invention

  ✓ Generate a great deal of support for your argument through invention and research so that you will have plenty to say, and your argument will move easily from point to point. In addition, it is always easier to refine and cut information as you move toward your final draft than to add information and sources as due dates close in.
  ✓ Concentrate on putting your ideas on the page during your first few drafts. Don't worry about punctuation and grammar. In later stages you can look for the kind of sentence-level errors that lead to awkwardness.

- Audience

  ✓ Research your audience's expectations so that you can deal with them effectively. If your professor is an electrical engineer, she may expect you to think and write like an electrical engineer. If you are writing a lab report, you should use the passive voice ("the beakers were filled" instead of "I filled the beakers") when describing the methods and materials used during an experiment because the doer of the action is not the primary focus. Professors from other disciplines, such as literature, will find the passive voice awkward.
  ✓ Assume that your audience members are expert detectors of logical fallacies as well as professional proofreaders. Of course, most of your readers will not be either of these things, but by taking a rigorous approach to editing and proofreading, you will be able to focus on the kinds of problems that lead to an awkward reading experience.
  ✓ Use transitions such as "in addition," "consequently," and "nevertheless" to smooth your readers' way. Remember, your audience members are reading or hearing your argument for the first time. Transitions will help them see how your ideas are connected and will make your argument flow. For example, in the following review of *Star Wars: The Force Awakens*, Stephen Marche explains how the movie is connected to previous episodes. Then he uses the transition "more importantly" to emphasize what sets the new episode apart from the others.

  > There are whole chunks of the movie which are direct inheritances from the first trilogy: ice worlds, desert planets, and, not to give too much away, something like a death star, only bigger.

More importantly, Abrams and the rest haven't forgotten what was so lacking from the prequel trilogy: a mythic substructure to the narrative.

The best transition not only says what is coming next but also indicates *why* the next subject or new idea is being introduced. Again, you know why, but your readers need to know, so tell them in a transition.

✓ Research your audience's thinking, beliefs, and behaviors just as you research your subject and counter-arguments. An understanding of your audience will help you make editorial decisions during the revision stage that convey a sense of authority in the mind of your audience.

- Authority

✓ Use what you know of your audience. Writers who successfully pitch screenplay ideas to studio executives make the types of editorial decisions that come from researching their audience. Though a writer may be excited to talk about her creative project, the studio exec is more interested in its financial potential. If a writer can frame the pitch in a way that indicates the potential profit of the screenplay, her audience will experience the kind of flow that comes from someone who knows how to make pitches—in other words, an authoritative voice.

✓ As you draft, have a friend, peer, classmate, or your professor read your draft, and ask your reader to identify places that are awkward or difficult to follow.

✓ Record yourself reading your draft aloud, or ask a friend to read it to you. Anytime there is a pause during reading, something does not sound right, or the paragraph leaves you hanging with more questions, odds are that is where you should begin to look for errors or better ways of expressing your ideas.

✓ Plan for thorough editing and proofreading. Editorial choices and errors such as the following can result in awkward writing that can lead a reader to question a writer's authority:
  ◉ errors in spelling
  ◉ odd word choice
  ◉ too many words (wordiness)
  ◉ punctuation errors
  ◉ grammar errors
  ◉ strange or unexpected sentence structure
  ◉ repetitive sentence structures
  ◉ repetitive sentence length
  ◉ breakdowns in paragraph structure
  ◉ paragraphs that are too long or too short
  ◉ logical fallacies

When audiences read or listen to public arguments, they expect correctness, and professors of any discipline will expect you to be as attentive to details like spelling and sentence structure as they are.

✓ If your writing seems wordy or the structure of a sentence seems wrong or hard to follow, find the skeletal sentence—the basic subject-verb structure—and then determine if you need fewer or additional words to modify or expand the idea in the sentence.

For example, an early draft of a Jameson book review may include the following wordy, hard-to-follow paragraph:

> Jameson begins with the idea that visual images are pornographic in his introduction. The goal, in other words, of visual images like photos and films, which is a recent focus of Jameson's work, is to provoke fascination and, if you think about how a visual image works instead of what an image shows, you are caught in the fascination of a visual image. In fact, films that are more abstract, such as black and white films like *Ballast* about the Mississippi Delta or Pixar's *Wall-E* are more about what they do not show or tell.

Highlighting the skeletal sentences, though, reveals the most basic meaning:

> **Jameson begins with the idea that visual images are pornographic** in his introduction. The goal, in other words, of **visual images** like photos and films, which is a recent focus of Jameson's work, is to **provoke fascination** and, **if you think about how a visual image works** instead of what an image shows, **you are caught in the fascination of a visual image**. In fact, **films that are** more **abstract**, such as black and white films like *Ballast* about the Mississippi Delta or Pixar's *Wall-E* **are** more **about what they do not show or tell**.

Once you have the skeletal sentence, you can decide on what additional information your audience will need to understand your meaning, and what you can leave out. For example, a revision of the skeletal meaning above may look like this:

> Visual images, for Jameson, are pornographic because they provoke fascination. Wondering how an image works as opposed to what an image shows and thinking about what is not shown are examples of the ways images fascinate.

✓ Look for sentences that begin with the same introductory clause or word. Repetition may sometimes be necessary and effective, but it can also lead to an experience of awkwardness. For example, the Declaration of Independence has 17 paragraphs that begin with "He has...." The 17 paragraphs are intended to demonstrate "repeated injuries and usurpations" by King George and provide overwhelming evidence supporting the decision to declare independence. However, in a research paper, such repetition can be tiresome to read, can diminish the impact of the points that follow, and can be an indication of an overly simple argument.

✓ Pay attention to sentence variety. As you develop your ideas, you may find yourself varying the lengths of your sentences without even thinking about it. When you review your work, though, look for and revise passages with a number of sentences of the same length or structure, which can be mind-numbing.

✓ Use appropriate sentence lengths to add authority to your argument. A long sentence can help you focus on the parts of a big or complex idea. You may have noticed that the definitions that follow a bold term in these chapters are often quite long. A medium-length sentence is the workhorse of a paragraph, but it can also be a counterpoint to longer or shorter sentences. A short sentence can emphasize a point, add dramatic effect, or indicate speed.

✓ Focus on a busy reader who is skeptical. What would make such a person slow down or stop reading? Sometimes making sure your writing has authority is as simple as remembering that even though your argument makes sense to you, you are not your audience. And never assume that your audience will be able to guess what you are thinking.

- What is overly complicated that needs to be defined, explained, or put in context so the reader can understand?
- What more needs to be said before you can move to your next point?
- Does the reader know why you are using a source and how the source supports or is related to the argument?
- Does the reader know why you think the source is authoritative? Should you add information about a source's credentials?

✓ Do not fall in love with any of your sentences or think that any sentence is too perfect to be cut.

MODULE VI-3

USING VISUALS IN YOUR ARGUMENT

A **visual** is an image, illustration, display, or graph used to communicate data, ideas, or emotions. **Visual conventions** are the elements of a visual that an audience expects in a given situation. These elements make communicating with a visual efficient and the data, ideas, or emotions more appealing or useful.

Visuals are effective. A study in the journal *Public Understanding of Science* found that readers are more likely to be persuaded by visual images such as graphs than by text or speech alone. Why? Visuals communicate a sense of authority, a connection to science, or an urgency that captures audience members' attention. Visuals catch a reader's eye, and if they are well designed and based on solid research, they can have the persuasive power of a longer written argument.

You can use visuals to create *logos*, *pathos*, and *ethos* appeals.

- *Logos* appeal. Graphs and charts give the impression of logical reasoning and can persuade your audience of the logic of your argument.
- *Pathos* appeal. Moving pictures and images, such as a hungry child or a soldier in the middle of a firefight, can provoke and link strong emotions to your argument.
- *Ethos* appeal. Framing and point of view can suggest or emphasize authority, wisdom, or leadership (Figure 6.6).

Figure 6.6
Statues of a nation's leaders are typically larger than life, forcing the viewer to look up. Such an *ethos* appeal is created by perspective rather than by words.

Creating Effective Visuals: General Guidelines

An argument can be composed primarily of visuals, like the following infographic showing Canadians' views on what it means to be a citizen (Figure 6.7). Or writers or speakers can use visuals such as line graphs or pie charts to support a claim in a text or as part of a speech. Photographers, graphic designers, painters, and information designers keep the following guidelines in mind as they create effective persuasive visuals.

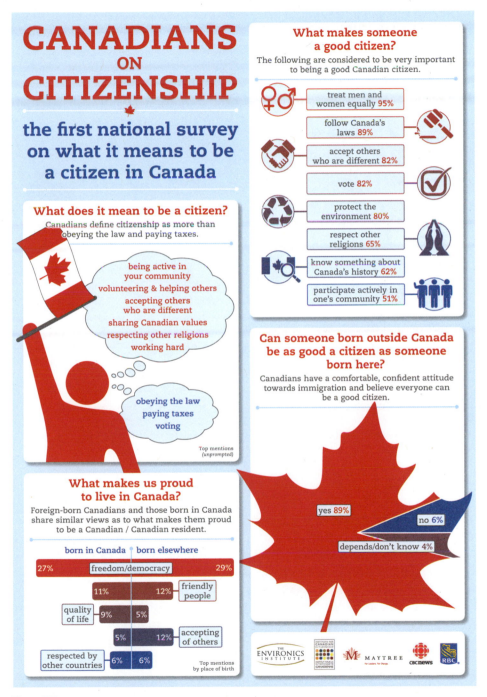

Figure 6.7
This infographic showing Canadians' views on citizenship is composed of six visual panels.

Keep it easy to understand. Whether you are using a graph or an image, simple is best, especially if your visual will be incorporated in a written text. For example, which is easier to understand in Figure 6.8, **A** or **B**?

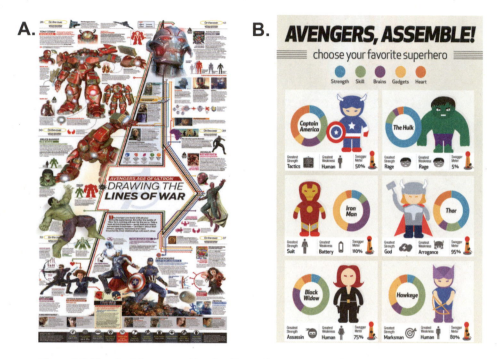

Figure 6.8 Visually, A is more exciting, but B organizes textual and visual information in an easy to understand format.

A visual that is part of a written or spoken argument must communicate a single idea or point. The idea or point may be complex, but it must hold together in the same way in which a paragraph is held together by a single idea or point. Visual B shows that the Avengers are a group of individuals with remarkable, distinct powers that come together to do more than a single individual could. This idea is communicated by organizing the diverse characteristics of each Avenger using five specific **variables** (qualities, numbers, or values) as criteria.

When composing a chart, you need to shape your visual for your purpose and avoid overloading your reader's ability to process information. For example, Visuals A and B in Figure 6.9 illustrate social media sharing on the web. Which one communicates its ideas more efficiently?

The answer depends upon your purpose. If you are focusing on how the top four social media sites compare, Visual A is better. If you want to communicate the complexity of social media sharing—a single idea—then B is the better graphic.

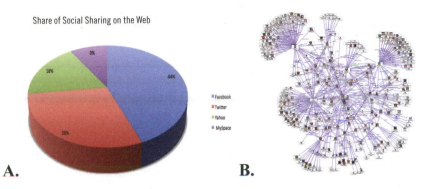

Figure 6.9 The pie chart (Visual A) and the node-link chart (Visual B) both provide information about sharing patterns in social media.

However, keep in mind that while the variables in Visual A are easy to understand quickly, the massive number of variables in Visual B may not be understood fully unless the reader stops to study the chart.

Use the composition of the image to convey meaning. Lines have traditionally been used to communicate different meanings and sensations within images. Your audience may expect you to use these same conventions.

- Diagonal lines convey speed, movement, and dynamic scenes.
- Horizontal lines suggest quiet, calm, pastoral scenes.
- Vertical lines convey a sense of tradition, permanence, upward movement, and optimism in a scene.

The arrows in the images in Figure 6.10 show the dominant direction and movement of each image. Effective visual arguments use direction and movement to communicate meaning and direct the viewers' eyes, so pick images that express the effect and meaning you intend.

Figure 6.10 The arrows have been added to highlight the graphic direction and movement within each image.

Use colors to convey meaning. Like composition, colors also communicate emotions, ideas, and sensations:

- Red suggests strong emotions: passion, energy, and violence.
- Blue offers a sense of calm, stability, faith, and purity.
- Green conveys power, ambition, security, and growth.

Authoritative groups and websites, such as the Graphic Artists Guild, can help you explore the meanings of colors and shapes.

Like rhetorical conventions, the conventional connotations of colors are reflected in our expectations and in how we read images. Specific audiences will read specific colors and color combinations in predictable ways. For example, royal purple and old gold means just one thing in Baton Rouge: Louisiana State University. For city dwellers, bright red and blue can bring to mind an emergency or crisis, but if you are a plumber, red is hot and blue is cold.

Black and white images can also communicate distinct meanings. Because a lack of color removes some context, black and white may give the impression of timelessness or endurance. A color image, on the other hand, is more engaging and easier to understand because most people see in color, color images capture context, and color suggests a contemporary setting. As a result, black and white images have a distant, objective feel, while color images seem more vibrant and immediate.

Frame your visuals to direct your reader. Scope is the context of your argument, such as an academic discipline. Within that scope, you have a **focus**, the position or specific proposition you want your reader or listener to accept and adopt.

When you are creating a visual to support your argument, you can use scope and focus to direct your readers' or viewers' eyes to important information, while providing the context that helps them understand what you want them to see. For example, in the original infographic in Figure 6.11, graphic designer and infographic artist Stephen Wildish used bright green and red to direct the viewer to look first at the center of his Euler diagram which is a variation of a Venn diagram. He used less vibrant colors to encourage the viewer to move out and around the diagram to consider the relationship between different dietary preferences or restrictions.

Adjust the frame of your visual to reflect your purpose. Visuals can be shaped to direct the reader's or viewer's eye just as a paragraph or essay directs the reader's thinking. For example, both Visual A and Visual B in Figure 6.12 represent the same information—the appearance of the words "manifest destiny" and "exceptionalism" in English language literature scanned by Google Books. If you wanted readers or

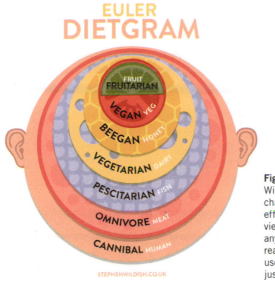

Figure 6.11
Wildish's image is charming, and it is effective because the viewer can begin reading anywhere, take in and read the entire image, or use the information from just a few parts.

viewers to compare the lack of these two words in literature from the seventeenth to the eighteenth centuries to their increasing presence in the nineteenth and twentieth centuries, Visual A would be a better choice. If your focus was the nineteenth and twentieth centuries alone, Visual B would be better because it directs the viewer's focus to the appearance of these words during that time.

Keep in mind that dishonest writers can manipulate visuals and graphs to distract or deceive. Module II-6 shows you how to check a source for its honesty. You can use the same principles to determine if you have misrepresented or unfairly manipulated the information and sources you use in a visual.

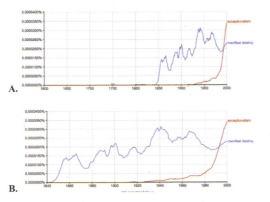

Figure 6.12
Two visuals tracking the appearance of "manifest destiny" and "exceptionalism" in English language literature.

Use point of view to highlight your focus. Your perspective, or the position from which you view an object, is your **point of view**.

Point of view can be created with the shot angle, lighting, framing, and positioning of elements within an image. For example, notice how the lighting and positioning directs your eye in the two images in Figure 6.13. In Image A, Aung San Suu Kyi, chairperson of the National League for Democracy in Myanmar, is highlighted and centered in a down shot, giving the appearance of separation, if not isolation, in a crowd as she prepares to cast a vote in Myanmar's first free election. Unlike Image A, in which the photographer's perspective appears distant from the subject, Image B is taken in the midst of Black Friday shopping with a level shot. The image centers on the chaotic pile of boxes, making them an overwhelming presence in the image.

Figure 6.13 Point of view in a photograph is determined by the location of the camera lens as well as the lighting and framing.

You can also create point of view in graphics. For example, it is almost impossible to ignore the center of the Euler type Venn diagram in Figure 6.11 because the compelling green and red colors and the arrangement of the circles creates a central focal point. In addition, you can use **negative space**, or the space surrounding the subject of the visual, to shape how an audience sees and understands information. Notice how framing creates empty or negative space in the graph in Figure 6.15 and how this space affects the way you understand the graph's information. How a graph is structured can shape an audience's understanding. Figure 6.7 is composed of many different graphs, but the up-and-down organization moves the reader to consider the first point in the visual argument before moving down to the next.

How you create and use an image will reflect a point of view that your reader will attach to you and your argument. Like any rhetorical device or strategy, you must be careful to use images in a way that contributes to your authority. Though it is easy to manipulate images and graphs, as the Responsible Sourcing box entitled "Honesty Is Authoritative" shows, your audience measures your authority based on how you use textual and visual sources.

Responsible Sourcing
Honesty Is Authoritative

In September 2009, *Newsweek* published this image of former Vice President Dick Cheney stabbing a bloody piece of meat. The image was cropped from a larger photo that showed his family clearing away dishes after a meal. Cropping provides a different, and possibly menacing, view of Cheney, whereas the fuller image portrays him as a family man.

In 2010, an *Economist* cover appeared to show a lonely President Barack Obama considering the damage to the Gulf of Mexico caused by the BP oil spill. However, the original image showed Obama being briefed by a Coast Guard admiral and a parish president on a much sunnier day than the cropped, darkened, and scrubbed image portrays.

As these two examples demonstrate, data and images are easily misrepresented when you change the scale of a graph, crop an image, or use tools like Photoshop. Prior to digital photography, dimming and scrubbing a photo would have taken a darkroom full of equipment, extensive expertise, and hours of work. As a result, there was time to consider whether altering a photo was worth the effort and expense and whether such changes were ethical. Now images can be altered on a smart-phone with a few swipes. However, keep in mind that the ability to change the composition of a photo does not mean that it is ethical to do so.

The same principles that guide you when you are quoting, summarizing, or paraphrasing a source also apply to the visuals you use. If you use only a portion of a photo or, for example, one panel from Heather Jones's visual argument (Figure 6.7), don't manipulate it in a way that alters its intended meaning. Always provide context and background that will help the reader understand the original circumstances in which the photo was taken or the graphic was presented. Make sure your documentation is accurate, and assume your audience will check to determine if you were responsible when documenting your source.

Types of Visuals

Different types of visuals communicate different messages in different ways. A photo can tell a story at a glance, and a graph can break down massive amounts of complex data into a simple presentation. The type of visual you use must deliver your message effectively for your intended audience so you can achieve your purpose.

Images. Images are representations of people, places, or items in the form of photos, drawings, or cartoons. Images typically portray a scene and can include individuals or items. As a result, they are especially effective at communicating narratives. For example, documentary images made by photojournalists, such as those in the Responsible Sourcing box, portray an occurrence or event. A landscape can tell the story of a location and impart a sense of what it is like to be there. A portrait can connect a face with a name, or it can function as a character study, revealing moods and dispositions.

Charts. A **chart** is a visual representation of data, data sets, or data trends. Timelines, bar graphs, line graphs, and pie charts are the most common types of charts. Each presents relationships among data in a different way.

- **Timelines** sequence information chronologically to highlight influences, effects, and events over time (Figure 6.14).
- **Bar graphs** portray significant differences in subjects that are being compared (Figure 6.15).
- **Line graphs** portray small changes over time, and they are most effective when portraying one trend (Figure 6.16) or at most a few trends over time.
- **Pie charts** are useful when you are comparing parts of a whole or elements within a single data set (Figure 6.17).

Figure 6.14
The history of hip-hop artists and musical styles is portrayed in this vertical time line.

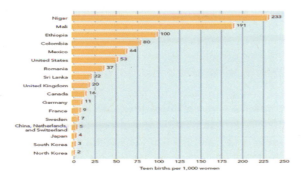

Figure 6.15
The bar graph compares birth rates in different countries.

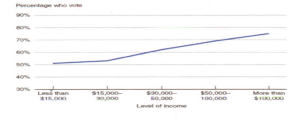

Figure 6.16
Probability of voting is graphed against income in this line graph.

Figure 6.17
The energy use of four sectors is shown in this pie chart.

There are many other ways to tell the story of relationships found in data, including Euler and Venn diagrams (Figure 6.11), node link charts (Figure 6.9B), and **word clouds** (Figure 6.18). These options can help an audience understand data trends and comparisons. Chart templates can be downloaded from sites such as Tableau Public and developed using software provided by TimeFlow, and Excel. Word clouds can be produced on sites such as WordItOut.com.

Figure 6.18
The most frequently used words in the first two paragraphs of this Module (p.162) are larger in this word cloud.

Information graphics. Information graphics, often called infographics, are composed of images, graphs, and text that communicate brief, coherent arguments, assertions, or facts in an easily accessible and beautiful way. The visuals in Figures 6.7, 6.8, 6.11, and 6.14 are infographics. You can easily find all kinds of infographics on the web, and the site Information Is Beautiful is an excellent source of compelling infographics. (Images you find, especially infographics, must be documented, as the Responsible Sourcing box entitled "Visuals Have Sources" explains.) You can also make your own infographics using software provided by sites such as Easelly, Google Developers, or Piktochart. Infographics are most effective when dealing with data that require a number of graphs or charts to illustrate. In addition, infographics that describe a process or hierarchy, like a flowchart, can also be useful. When deciding whether to use an infographic, consider your audience's expectations and the common practices of the situation you are in.

Maps. Maps organize information geographically. For example, a topographical map locates, names, and shows relationships between elevation changes, geological formations like hills and canyons, and built places like towns. There are many types of maps. A dot distribution map places dots on a geographic map to represent data, numbers, or values (Figure 6.19). Maps of all types can be downloaded from sources such as GeoCommons or produced using software suites such as Google Maps API.

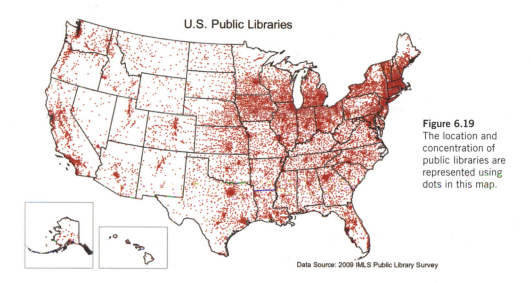

U.S. Public Libraries

Figure 6.19
The location and concentration of public libraries are represented using dots in this map.

Data Source: 2009 IMLS Public Library Survey

Responsible Sourcing
Visuals Have Sources

Visuals that are presented without a source are suspicious, while visuals that include information about a source trusted by your audience are persuasive. Not only does a source note—presented and formatted in a style expected by your audience—have persuasive power, but the authority of that source also contributes to the authority of your argument.

In an academic setting, when your audience is a professor or fellow class-mates, you must include the source of any visual you use. In addition, if you are using a visual found online, you must acknowledge the copyright of the author or creator of the visual.

For more information on why citing sources is necessary and how accurate in-text citations, bibliographies, and works-cited pages contribute to your authority, see Module II-7, II-8, and Chapter 7. Fair use allows scholars to use words, sound clips, and images created by others for academic purposes without formally requesting permission. However, fair use is not a license to use another person's work without properly acknowledging the source. For help with documenting sources, including visuals, by correctly using MLA or APA style, see Chapter 7.

Use Relevant Visuals

To be effective, visuals should be relevant, enhance your authority, and support the appeals of your argument. You know what the image you are using portrays and why it is in your text, but will your audience know? When selecting or creating images, keep these guidelines in mind.

- Charts and other visuals communicate authority only if they are directly related to your argument and the source of the data portrayed is easily understood. The meaning of a complex graphic may be clear to you, but what matters is whether your audience understands it.
- Images can help you describe a scene or an object or to analyze or compare objects with small, subtle, or nuanced qualities or differences. For example, an effective screen shot can supplement, or even replace, a detailed description in the text.
- Avoid cliché images, and do not use images as filler to meet a page minimum: both options are obvious and undercut your authority. For example, clip art, emoticons, and images of sunsets or animal gifs may be fun, but they distract from your subject and authority.
- Used strategically, an image or a graph can also create a pause in a text or a transition from one point to the next. For example, let's say you were writing a research paper on the evolution of rap music. After a discussion of bling rap of the late 1990s, you are ready to move on to part two of your analysis, the emerging hipster hop movement. Visualizing the transition between the two subjects in some way could help your audience follow your argument.

MODULE VI-4

USING DESIGN CONVENTIONS IN YOUR ARGUMENT

Back when newspapers, magazines, and books were the primary media, accepted ways of using texts and visuals were determined by professional editors and designers. Times have changed: third graders can now use Evernote, Photoshop, and Google Docs to produce slick-looking class journals. Multimedia chapbooks and PowerPoint or Prezi presentations are common assignments in universities and colleges. Still, many of the conventions that audiences expect and find helpful have remained relatively constant. In fact, when readers move through a traditional print or digital presentation, they have similar expectations for the use of text, space, and images.

Textual Conventions

Textual conventions are language and formatting practices that writers, speakers, and their intended audiences have agreed upon and accepted. Some groups, such as the Associated Press, Wikipedia, and American Horse Publications, formalize their conventions in stylebooks. Even Badoo and Twitter have informal, accepted language practices. On most social networks, you learn the accepted style by watching how people successfully engage one another and by their mistakes.

In an academic setting, conventions may include expectations about margin width, the content of headers and footers, the use and placement of visuals, in-text source citations and lists of sources, footnotes or endnotes, spelling and punctuation, and fonts. Imagine the one research paper in a stack of 40 that has different margins than all the rest. Such a paper will stand out, and probably not in a good way.

If you are composing an argument outside of college, following the textual conventions your audience expects will contribute to your authority. Your readers or listeners may not even be aware of the conventions they use as markers of authority, but they can recognize when something is off. Imagine THE WALL STREET JOURNAL. banner in a different font. Imagine *Time* magazine without its signature red border. Conventions can help you recognize authority, and playing with conventions can help your work stand out.

Some conventions, like those for spelling and punctuation, are consistent across most writing situations. Other textual conventions—such as margin width, the use of personal pronouns, and the correct placement of visuals—can vary depending on the audience or the academic discipline.

Many professors give detailed descriptions of the conventions they expect you to follow in writing prompts or assignment sheets, or they may indicate that you should follow the conventions explained in the handbook they require you to buy. If your professor does not tell you the conventions to use in your writing, ask which standard style, such as that recommended by the Modern Language Association (MLA) or the American Psychological Association (APA), they prefer. Most academic style manuals also include detailed instructions concerning margin width, documentation, spelling and punctuation, and even the best fonts to use. (For more on MLA and APA style, see Chapter 7.)

Everything you read either upholds conventions or breaks them; intentionally or unintentionally. Writers who make the most effective use of visuals and text do so by making their choices about conventions, techniques, and visuals both effective and invisible to the reader. For example, most readers won't know which font a writer is using, but a font that is difficult to read can affect the writer's authority nevertheless.

Fonts or **typefaces** are styles or designs of letters. Some fonts are designed to be easy to read and some are designed to provoke an emotion or send a message, such as the constancy, power, and authority expressed by the *Wall Street Journal*'s banner font. On paper, serif fonts, with tiny tails at the ends of certain letters, appear to aid readers' comprehension more than sans serif fonts, which do not have tails. Most electronic texts are sans serif because making the little tails and feet legible on all screens with different resolution rates is difficult.

Serif
Courier
Times New Roman
Garamond

San Serif
Arial
Calibri
Verdana

Your professor may indicate a preferred font. If not, use the simplest font, keeping in mind that all editorial choices, including which font to use, can enhance or damage your authority.

Spatial Conventions

Though the term "spatial conventions" may sound theoretical, in fact you encounter these conventions every day. For example, we expect rooms to be furnished and hallways to be plain. A hallway cluttered with chairs and bookcases would seem as odd as an office with no desk or chair. Spatial conventions for texts involve the way in which linear text, like the lines of words in this paragraph, is organized and presented, the composition of an image, or the ways in which a graph and text are arranged.

Layout refers to how you place images and texts on a page, poster, or slide. Good layout helps the audience move smoothly through your pages and slides and contributes to the persuasive power of your argument, whereas poor layout is confusing or leads to questions such as "What is that graph supposed to mean?"

Think about how audiences move through your text. Each genre is shaped differently, depending on readers' expectations and the medium in which it appears. If your argument is a web page, composed of text and visuals, for example, think about how your audience will scroll through such a text.

Research that tracks readers' eye movements shows that people typically move through a web page in an F pattern. English speaking readers start at the top left of a page or section reading from left to right and work their way down. However, the farther down a page they go, the more likely they are to skip words or images on the right side. As Figure 6.20 shows, those reading web pages with narrow columns (left image) of text have narrow F patterns compared to pages where the text runs from the left edge to the right edge (right image). Also, web pages with visuals (center image) show the same F pattern as pages of text alone. All three eye-tracking maps of the different web pages show that the text or images at the bottom right received almost no attention.

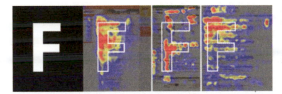

Figure 6.20 Areas where a viewer's eyes were focused for the longest time or most frequently are framed by the letter F. Areas outside the F are rarely noticed by the reader.

Layout techniques are based on how audiences move through documents, pages, websites, and presentation slides. Web usability consultant Jakob Nielsen tells his clients to build their web pages with the most important images and information in the top left, and always to assume that the first few lines of a section or paragraph will have the most impact. Readers place less value on information and images farther down or farther to the right of the screen.

The following techniques will help you lay out the visuals and text of your argument:

- **Determine the types of layouts your audience expects**. For example, if you have to give a class presentation in a business class, you might ask your professor for examples from previous classes so you can see how those students laid out their argument efficiently.
- **Use the layout templates that PowerPoint and Prezi provide**. Microsoft and Prezi both provide video tutorials that show you how to lay out slides and build presentations.
- **Incorporate visuals at points where they can be useful**. Include your visuals when you outline a multimedia argument. In this way, you can see where you may need visuals and where you have too many.
- **Be consistent**. If all your graphs are in rich colors except for one, your audience will wonder why. Such inconsistencies should be avoided if possible, or explained if intentional.
- **Indicate importance by size**. If all your visuals are equally important or of the same type, they should be the same size. If your argument ends with a passionate call to action, a tiny motivating image would work against the mood or need you are trying to establish.

Tie visuals to your text. Your audience will not make the connection between your argument and a visual that supports it if you don't, or they will make a connection that is different from what you intended. When you use images or graphs in your argument, therefore, you need to do the following:

- Introduce each visual individually.
- Discuss the relevance of the visual to your immediate point and your overall argument.
- Duplicate or represent the data and image honestly.
- Locate your image or graph above or just after the point you are trying to illustrate, unless the style you are using requires a different placement.
- Avoid separating images and the text that discusses them. For example, if a graph is on page 10, the analysis of the graph's data should not be on page 9 or 11.
- Include a caption to help readers know what they are looking at in an image. ·

Captions are brief titles or descriptions of a visual located immediately below the visual. Your caption should provide enough information for your audience to understand the image or graph. In addition, your caption should be in the same style as the text, it should be brief, and it should support your argument. Ideally, a caption identifies relevant individuals, activities, processes, or items in the image. If you have multiple visuals or refer to the same visual at different times during your argument, your caption should include a number, like the figure numbers in this chapter.

MODULE VI-5

PROOFREADING YOUR ARGUMENT

Proofreading should be your final step before turning in any type of assignment. Once you have made larger editorial decisions and are satisfied with how your text flows and that your visuals are working, you should proofread for mechanical errors. It may seem unfair or petty, but audiences judge the intellect and competency of authors or speakers by their accuracy, polish, and attention to detail. For professors and other readers, a 5-page paper with no errors may have more persuasive power than a carefully researched 10-page paper with mistakes on every page. Because readers of all types put such value on correctness, and a flawless paper or talk enhances authority, writers and public speakers turn to professional proofreaders like Naomi Long Eagleson.

Long Eagleson has four rules that she keeps in mind when proofreading:

1. Work from a printed text on paper to see small punctuation marks and letters more clearly.
2. Temporarily change the font type, type size, and/or color you are using. Seeing your work anew will give you fresh eyes to spot the hidden errors.

3. Focus like a ninja by using a ruler to cover the line below the one you are scanning for errors.
4. You will rarely go wrong with using the Oxford comma. An **Oxford comma** is the second comma in a sequence of three words or phrases, or the comma before the word "and" that leads to the final element of a longer series:

> I traveled to Maine, Georgia, and Florida during the summer.

Journalists, however, do not use the Oxford comma.

The following checklist will also help you build and protect your authoritative voice as you proofread.

- Schedule time for proofreading

✓ Just as you set aside time to write, set aside time to proofread.
✓ Proofread each page at least three times, including cover pages and lists of works cited or references. For example, if it takes you five minutes to proofread a single page carefully and you are planning to proofread three different times, you should be prepared to set aside 1 hour and 15 minutes for proofreading a five-page paper.
✓ Take a break between proofreading sessions. Careful proofreading requires concentration, and the longer you do it the less able you will be to focus.

- Get help

✓ Peers, friends, and classmates can help you proofread. You don't have to be a professional like Long Eagleson to find errors. All you or your reviewers need is time to read and a sense of what doesn't sound right and what seems wrong.
✓ Don't assume that your readers have caught everything or that their advice is always correct. Even if you have run spell check and grammar check three times and had four friends read and correct your errors, *you* still need to go through it and make the decisions to revise sentences or fix typos yourself. If you don't understand an error that a peer reviewer has pointed out, don't make a change until you understand how to correct it.
✓ Most campus writing centers, learning centers, or tutors will not proofread your paper for you. However, they will work with you on your text, explaining why a word, sentence, or paragraph needs your attention. In this way, they are teaching you how to proofread: skills that will help you in all your classes and in the other types of writing you will do.

- Develop and stick to a proofreading strategy

✓ Always start with major problems and work your way to smaller issues. For example, the first time you proofread, you might focus only on transitions between paragraphs and captions beneath images. The second time you might decide to focus only on punctuation and word choice or usage. Finally, for your last reading you would focus only on spelling. In addition, if in the past you have had trouble with transitions and using commas in a series of three, you should prioritize those types of errors.

✓ Trick your mind into seeing your paper anew. You may have noticed that it is easier to find errors in someone else's paper than in your own. Because you have worked on your paper so long and read it so many times, you will tend to correct your mistakes automatically while reading it. You can trick your brain with this simple process:

  ⊚ Start reading at the last sentence, and read it for a specific error type, like punctuation mistakes.

  ⊚ Go to the second last sentence, and read it for the same type of mistakes.

Reading in this way will help you focus on mechanical errors like sentence problems and incorrect or missing commas.

CHAPTER 7
DOCUMENTATION

MODULE VII-1

MLA STYLE FOR IN-TEXT CITATIONS

The documentation style recommended by the Modern Language Association, called **MLA style**, is used by disciplines in the humanities and liberal arts. MLA provides the definitive, or official, guidelines for this style in the *MLA Handbook, 9th edition*, published in 2021.

As with any documentation system, the purpose of following the MLA style is to link the words, work, or ideas of others that you use in your argument to the original sources. The MLA style is composed of brief citations within the text that point to a list of works cited with full bibliographic information.

In-text citations, sometimes referred to as *parenthetical citations* because they are often enclosed in parentheses, appear in the body of an essay, immediately after or before material from a source that has been integrated into the text. In-text citations provide just enough information for a reader to find the source in the works-cited list, as shown in Figure 7.1. The list of **works cited** is arranged in alphabetical order at the end of an essay. Each entry provides the who, what, where, and when information needed to find a source using any library, search engine, or database.

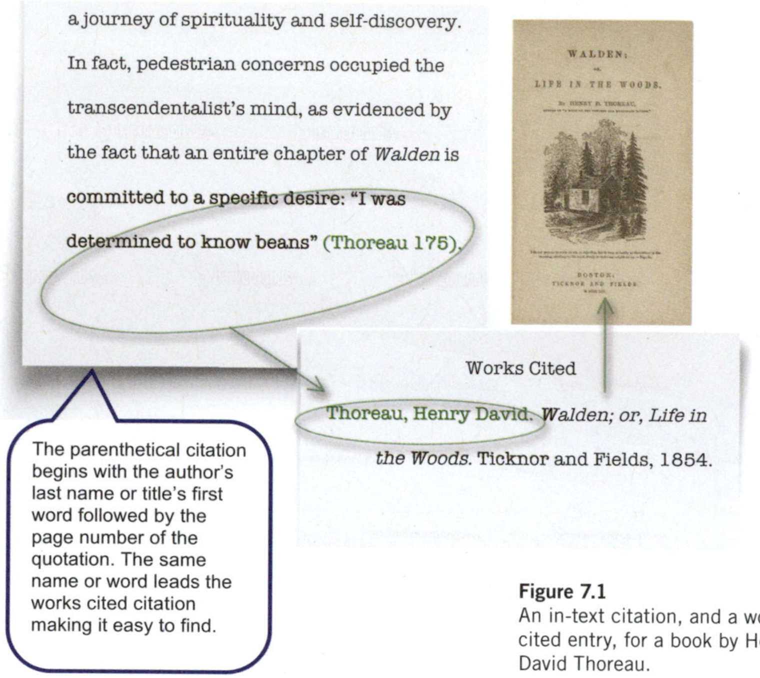

a journey of spirituality and self-discovery.

In fact, pedestrian concerns occupied the

transcendentalist's mind, as evidenced by

the fact that an entire chapter of *Walden* is

committed to a specific desire: "I was

determined to know beans" (Thoreau 175).

WALDEN;
or,
LIFE IN THE WOODS.

By HENRY D. THOREAU.

BOSTON:
TICKNOR AND FIELDS.

Works Cited

Thoreau, Henry David. *Walden; or, Life in the Woods*. Ticknor and Fields, 1854.

The parenthetical citation begins with the author's last name or title's first word followed by the page number of the quotation. The same name or word leads the works cited citation making it easy to find.

Figure 7.1
An in-text citation, and a works-cited entry, for a book by Henry David Thoreau.

In-Text Citations Focus on Who and Where

In-text citations are composed of the answer to the *who* question and a small bit of *where* information, such as page numbers, so that the reader can find where a quotation or piece of information is located within a source.

Identifying the author in an integrating phrase or sentence is the method of in-text citation preferred by most instructors and is a more effective way to incorporate information from a source than placing an author's name in the parenthetical citation. Examples 1, 3, and 5 below show how to integrate an author or authors in the text using signal phrases. If the author is not identified in the sentence that introduces or includes the information from the source, a parenthetical citation that includes the author's name is necessary. Examples 2, 4, and 6 place the author information in the parenthetical citation. Naming the author in the parenthetical citation may also help the reader when you are referring to more than one source in a single paragraph. (See Module II-8 for more on integrating sources into your text.)

Page numbers are uncommon in many electronic formats such as web pages. If you can find page numbers, use them in the parenthetical reference, following the author's or authors' name(s). If the author's or authors' name(s) appear in the integrating phrase or sentence, only the page number appears in parentheses. Think of the page number like a red pin on a Google map: they make things easier to find. Here are some simple tricks of the trade for using page and other numbers in parenthetical citations.

- When you are citing multiple pages that being with the same first number, use only the last two digits of the second, or ending number. For example, (Faulkner 571–78) actually means pages 571 to 578.
- If you are citing a work with many volumes or organized by parts and sections, that kind of additional information makes it easier to track down your source and can demonstrate your authority. For example, a parenthetical citation of *Robert's Rules of Order* that uses parts and articles might look like this: (Robert 185; pt. 2, art. 4).
- Many novels, poems, and plays are available in multiple editions, so other types of location information, such as book, chapter, act, scene, canto, line, or part, can be added to the page number or be used instead of page numbers:

> Lena does not resist her suitors, but suggests she is helpless against their interests when she says, "I can't order him off. It ain't my prairie" (Cather 94; bk. 2, ch. 4).

If you are using line numbers, do not include page numbers. Use line numbers only if provided by the source.

> And I a smiling woman.
> I am only thirty.
> And like the cat I have nine times to die. (Plath, lines 19–21)

- If you are referring to an entire work, such as a book or an article, you do not need to use page numbers.

Example In-Text Citations

1. One author identified in an integrating sentence

Introducing a source and a brief explanation of its relevance to your argument is essential to building an authoritative voice. When you introduce the author of a source in your text, there is no need to repeat his or her name in parentheses. The page number, if it is available, is sufficient. If a page number is not available, the parenthetical citation is omitted.

> Willa Cather's sense of the lives of Nebraska farmers and the power of the land is captured by the narrator of *My Ántonia* when he thinks, "At any rate, that is happiness; to be dissolved into something complete and great" (14).

2. One author in a parenthetical citation
If you do not identify the author or authors in the integrating phrase or sentence, you must do so in the parenthetical citation. For individuals, use the last name only followed by the page number, with no intervening comma.

> "At any rate, that is happiness; to be dissolved into something complete and great" (Cather 14).

3. Two authors identified in an integrating sentence
Name both authors, connecting them with "and." The title of a work you are citing can also appear in the in-text reference, as shown here.

> James Watson and Francis Crick's article "A Structure for Deoxyribose Nucleic Acid" is renowned for first describing DNA as we know it today. It should also be celebrated for its humble tone—"It has not escaped our notice that the specific pairing we have postulated immediately suggests a possible copying mechanism for the genetic material" (737)—as well as its brevity.

4. Two authors in a parenthetical citation
The last name of both authors must be in the same order as listed in the original text.

> The essay that first described DNA as we know it today (Watson and Crick) is only 15 paragraphs long.

5. Three or more authors identified in an integrating sentence
When your source has three or more authors, use the last name of the first author listed and the abbreviation "et al.," which means "and others."

> In their study of predictive coding, Saygin et al. trace human responses to humanoid movement, and as they do so they appear to treat the humans they study as robots (413–16).

Whether you list all the names or use "et al.," the in-text citation must match the *who* information that begins the works-cited citation, or the reader will have difficulty finding it.

6. Three or more authors in a parenthetical citation
If your source is authored by three or more people, begin the citation with the first author's last name and the abbreviation "et al."

> Some cognitive researchers of human responses to robots treat humans as robots (Saygin et al. 413–16).

The name in the parenthetical citation must match the *who* information that begins the works-cited citation so that readers can make the connection to the works-cited list.

7. Group author identified in an integrating sentence

If a source produced by a group, such as a corporation or an organization, does not name individual authors, the group name appears in the in-text citation, following the pattern of example 1 (one author). Note that this citation does not include a page number because it is from a website.

> The California Dry Bean Advisory Board argues that it is almost impossible to meet the USDA's inspection standards for "insect webs and filth" in beans sold for human consumption.

8. Anonymous author in an integrating sentence

If a document, text, or work has no identifiable author, use the *what*—the title of the document, text, or work—to identify the source and connect it to the list of works cited.

> In "One More Punch," we are reminded that Ivermectin has been around since the 1980s (76).

9. Group author in a parenthetical citation

If a group or organization produced your source, use the first distinctive word or words in the group name to connect the source to the works-cited list. Since the following is a web-based source without numbered pages, page numbers are not included in the parenthetical reference.

> It is almost impossible to meet the USDA's inspection standards for "insect webs and filth" (California Dry Bean Advisory Board).

10. Anonymous author in a parenthetical citation

If the *who*, or author, information is not available or is listed as anonymous on the original source, then the *what* information—usually the title—will help your reader connect your source to the works-cited citation. If the title is brief, you may use it all. If the title is more than three words, use the first few distinct words of the title (not *a*, *an*, or *the*).

> As the November edition of *The Economist* points out, Ivermectin is powerful: "It has been known since the 1980s that the drug kills arthropods (ticks, mites, insects and so on) foolish enough to bite someone treated with it" ("One More" 76).

If, however, you happen to use two sources with similar titles, such as "One More Punch" and "One More Job for the CFO," then you need to use enough words from the titles to make it clear which you are referring to.

("One More Punch" 76).
("One More Job" 12).

MODULE VII-2

MLA LIST OF WORKS CITED

In MLA style, the list of works cited includes a single entry for each source cited within the text. Each entry provides detailed answers to the *who*, *what*, *where*, and *when* questions, allowing the reader to search for and locate the exact source you used.

Elements of Style for Works-Cited Citations

Works-cited page format. The works-cited list starts a new page with "Works Cited" as the centered title. Double-space each citation, and alphabetize each entry using the first important word of the citation (last name of the author or first-named author, group name, or title).

Sequence of elements. In the MLA style, the elements that answer the *who*, *what*, *where*, and *when* questions are always the same and almost always in the same order:

Author. Title of source. Title of the container, contributors, version, number, publisher's name, date of publication, location.

The concept of **containers**—simply where your source is found—was new to the eighth edition of the *MLA Handbook*. For example, if you are citing a poem in a collection such as an anthology, the anthology is the container. If you are citing a data set from a database or an article from a website, the database or website is the container for your source.

Different types of citations will use different elements. For example, the basic citation for a book uses only four elements:

Kerouac, Jack. *Big Sur.* Penguin, 1962.

Hanging indent. A hanging indent is the reverse of a normal indent. The first line begins at the margin, and all following lines of the same entry are indented one-half inch (about five spaces):

> Brassett, James. "British Irony, Global Justice: A Pragmatic Reading of Chris Brown, Banksy and Ricky Gervais." *Review of International Studies*, vol. 35, no. 1, 2009, pp. 219–45.

The author, authors, or authoring group begins the citation, if there is a named author, and the *who* information for each citation must connect to the name or names in the integrating phrase or sentence or be identical to the name or names in the parenthetical reference. The MLA lists names, groups, or the titles of anonymous texts in the same way for all types of documents, texts, and works, as shown in examples 1–6 below.

Example Works-Cited Citations for Different Types of Authorship

1. One author
Put the family name first, followed by first name and then any middle name or initial, as shown in the original source. Note that in the example below, "UP" is the standard and acceptable abbreviation for "University Press."

> Cather, Willa. *My Ántonia.* Oxford UP, 2009.

2. Two authors
Reverse the first author's name and list the second author as her or his name appears in the source: Last, First, First Last, and First Last, etc.

> Watson, James, and Francis Crick. "A Structure for Deoxyribose Nucleic Acid." *Nature*, vol. 171, 1953, pp. 737–38.

3. Three or more authors
In the same way in which three or more names are cited parenthetically in the text, use the abbreviation "et al."

Saygin, Ayse Pinar, et al. "The Thing That Should Not Be: Predictive Coding and the Uncanny Valley in Perceiving Human and Humanoid Robot Actions." *Social Cognitive and Affective Neuroscience*, vol. 7, no. 4, 2012, pp. 413–22.

4. A group author

Government documents and reports put out by corporations and other groups often list the group name, such as the Rand Corporation or the National Geospatial-Intelligence Agency, as the author. In such cases, the full name of the group is used and alphabetized based on the first important word in the name (not *a*, *an*, or *the*).

United States Department of Agriculture. "United States Standards for Beans." Federal Grain Inspection Service, 2005, p. 5, http://www.usdrybeans. com/wp-content/files/2011/08/US-Dry-Bean-Grading-Standards.pdf.

5. Anonymous author

If no author, of any kind, is identified by the source, skip the *who* information and begin the entry with the answer to *what*, that is, the title.

Diary of an Oxygen Thief. 2nd ed., V Publishing, 2009.

6. Two or more works by the same author

If you are citing two or more works by the same author, alphabetize the works using the first important word in each of the titles. The citation of the first book will invert the full name of the author as described in examples 1–3 above. The second and any subsequent works by the same author will begin with three hyphens and a period to indicate that the work is also produced by the same author.

Kerouac, Jack. *Big Sur.* Penguin Books, 1962.
---. *On the Road: The Original Scroll.* Edited by Howard Cunnell, Penguin Books, 2007.

Example Work-Cited Citations for Different Types of Sources

Works-cited citations vary greatly depending upon the *what* information they include, in part because documents, texts, and other works are available in so many different genres and media.

Below, you will find documentation models for the following broad types of sources:

- books
- periodicals, or sources published regularly

- interviews
- visuals
- audio, video, and broadcast sources
- online sources
- other digital sources.

Always cite the sources that you summarized, paraphrased, or quoted. Sometimes, you may lose the original documentation information and think that any version or edition of the source will do. However, such switches can only lead to trouble. Books or articles that have the same author and title can be very different in terms of editing and page numbers. For example, the Knopf edition of Toni Morrison's novel *The Bluest Eye* is 215 pages long, but the Vintage reprint is 224 pages long.

Books

7. Print book
The print citation sets the pattern for all citations of books.

> Kerouac, Jack. *Big Sur*. Penguin, 1962.

8. Book downloaded from an e-book publisher
Indicate the version and digital publisher, if any.

> Kerouac, Jack. *Big Sur*. Kindle ed., Devault-Graves Digital Editions, 2012.

Some digitally distributed books are read using your browser, so you do not need to download a copy. The following is an example from Google Books.

> Dickens, Charles. *Great Expectations*. Boston, 1881. *Google Books*, 2017,
>   play.google.com/books/reader?printsec=frontcover&output=reader&id
>   =fhUXAAAAYAAJ&pg=GBS.PA527.

9. An introduction, foreword, or afterword of a book
Begin the citation with the name of the person who wrote the introduction, foreword, or afterword. The full name of the author of the book follows the title of the book and the word "by," and the page number or numbers follows the date of publication. If the author wrote the element you are citing, include only the author's last name after "by." If no name is given, then you may assume the author of the book is also the author of the introduction, foreword, or afterword.

Fussell, Paul. Introduction. *The Road to Oxiana*, by Robert Byron, Oxford UP, 2007, pp. 9–16.

10. Book with an editor and/or translator

The names of an editor and or a translator are considered part of the *what* information and follow the title.

Kolmogorov, A.N. *Foundations of the Theory of Probability*. Translated and edited by Nathan Morrison, Chelsea Publishing, 1950.

11. A book with a volume or an edition number

A. A book with a volume number is one of a set of books that have the same title. Use "Vol." for the word "Volume."

Freud, Sigmund. *The Standard Edition of the Complete Psychological Works of Sigmund Freud*. Edited by James Strachey, vol. 7, Vintage, 2001.

B. An edition is a version of a book or one of many printings of a book. Use "ed." for the word "edition."

Diary of an Oxygen Thief. 2nd ed., V Publishing, 2009.

12. A work in an anthology or collection

Though anthologies or collections may have many contributors, such as the translator of a specific work or a general editor, the citation always begins with the author of the particular work you are citing.

De Man, Paul. "Semiology and Rhetoric." *Critical Theory: A Reader for Literary and Cultural Studies*, edited by Robert Dale Parker, Oxford UP, 2012, pp. 133–45.

Periodicals or Sources Published Regularly

13. An article in a scholarly journal

The articles in a scholarly journal are written by experts and scholars for the purpose of sharing experimental findings and the results of their research. Some journals are published monthly or quarterly; others are published every six months or every year. As a result, citations for articles in scholarly journals include more specific *where* information than books do, including the journal name, volume number, issue number, and inclusive page numbers for the article.

A. An article from a printed scholarly journal

Author   Title

Mortenson, Erik. "Capturing the Fleeting Moment: Photography in the Work
of Allen Ginsberg." *Chicago Review*, vol. 51, no. 1–2, 2005, pp. 215–31.

Journal Title   Date   Page numbers
Volume   Published
Issue

B. An article in an online scholarly journal is similar to a print article. However,
online articles often do not include page numbers. After giving the basic citation
information, include the DOI. A **DOI**, or digital object identifier, is a specific code
that provides an enduring link to a work that will not change or get lost. If you can't
find a DOI, use the URL web address (omitting the http://).

Lippit, Akira Mizuta. "David Lynch's Wholes." *Flow*, vol. 15, no. 3, 2011,
www.flowjournal.org/2011/11/david-lynchs-wholes/.

C. An article from an online database such as *JSTOR* or *ProQuest* must include the
name of the database and the DOI or URL of the article.

Jauss, Hans Robert. "Literary History as a Challenge to Literary Theory."
A Symposium on Literary History, vol. 2, no. 1, 1970, pp. 7–37. *JSTOR*,
https://doi:10.2307/468585.

14. Magazine
Magazine citations are similar to scholarly journal citations, but they lack volume
and issue numbers. Note the specific month or date of publication.

A. An article in a magazine published monthly

Mathews, Dana. "It's Austin Mahone's World and We're All Just Living in
It." *TeenVogue*, Dec. 2014/Jan. 2015, pp. 53–56.

B. An article in a magazine published weekly

Foroohar, Raina. "Starbucks for America." *Time*, 5 Feb. 2015, pp. 23–27.

C. An article from a magazine's online edition

> Peters, Mark. "*Felgercarb*: An Underused, Sci-Fi Word for BS." *Slate*, 5 Nov. 2015, www.slate.com/blogs/lexicon_valley/2015/11/05/mark_peters _bullshit_word_of_the_day_felgercarb_is_a_sci_fi_word_for_bs.html.

15. Newspaper
An article in a newspaper must indicate the edition and section and page numbers if they are available.

A. An article in a newspaper

> Musetto, Vincent. "Headless Body in Topless Bar." *New York Post*, final ed., 15 Apr. 1983, p. A1.

B. An article from a newspaper's online edition

Many newspapers have online editions. Include the date when the article was posted and its DOI or URL.

> Rocha, Veronica. "Arrest Made in Death of Transgender Woman after O.C. Silicone Party." *Los Angeles Times*, 9 Feb. 2015, www.latimes.com /local/lanow/la-me-ln-transgender-silicone-party-death-20150209 -story.html.

C. A review of a book or work

> Russo, Maria. "A Book that Started with Its Pictures: Ransom Riggs Is Inspired by Vintage Snapshots." *The New York Times*, 30 Dec. 2013, p. C1.

Government-Sponsored or Related Document

16. Government documents
A government document may have an individual author, or it may have authors affiliated with corporations or research centers. Or such documents may list only the government agency as the author. Also, it is possible for the publisher to be the same as the author, as in example A below. In that case, start with the title and list the organization as the publisher.

A. A printed government document

> *Report to the President.* Presidential Commission on the Space Shuttle Chal-
> lenger Accident, 6 June 1986. 5 vols.

It is not unusual to find a source with **no date of publication**. If you cannot find a
date, use the available evidence to make an informed guess and indicate your estimate with a question mark (for example 2009? or 18th century?).

B. A government document published online

> Daues, Jessica. "Lunar Maps Paved Way for Moon Exploration." *NGA
> Historical Collection*, National Geospatial-Intelligence Agency, 2009?
> www.nga.mil/About/History/Apollo%2011/Pages/default.aspx.

Interviews

Interview citations always begin with the name of the person answering the questions: the interviewee.

17. Interviews

A. A printed interview

> Derrida, Jacques. "'Eating Well,' or the Calculation of the Subject." *Points...:
> Interviews, 1974–1994*, edited by Werner Hamacher and David E. Well-
> bery, translated by Peter Connor and Avital Ronell, Stanford UP, 1995,
> pp. 255–77.

B. An interview from an online source

> Crumb, Robert. "R. Crumb: The Art of Comics No. 1." Interview by Ted
> Widmer. *The Paris Review*, no. 193, 2010, www.theparisreview.org
> /interviews/6017/the-art-of-comics-no-1-r-crumb.

C. A personal interview

If you interviewed someone, use "Interview with the author" and include the date
of the interview.

> Ryan, Dermot. Interview with the author, 14 Apr. 2017.

Visuals

18. Map or chart

Maps can be individual sheets but are commonly part of a book or atlas, such as example A below. A map citation provides the name of the creator or mapmaker and name of the map in the usual sequence. If no name is provided, give the map a title that would make it easy to identify and fits the context in which it was found. In addition, include the word "map" or "chart."

A. Print map

> Paullin, Charles O. "Settled Area 1760 and Population 1750." *Atlas of the Historical Geography of the United States*, edited by John K. Wright, Greenwood, 1975, p. 60. Map.

B. Online chart

> Federal Aviation Administration. "Omaha SOMA." FAA FFR Charts, 20 July 2017. Sectional aviation chart. aeronav.faa.gov/content/aeronav /tac_files/PDFs/Kansas_City_TAC_84_P.pdf. Accessed 28 Feb. 2018.

19. Work of art

A citation for a work of art such as a painting or sculpture begins with the creator and the title of the work. Then include the date it was created, the institution or collection where the work is housed, and the city. If the date is approximate, use "circa" (for example, circa 1450).

> Caravaggio, Michelangelo Merisi da. *The Conversion of St. Paul.* 1601, Odescalchi Balbi Collection, Rome.

20. Image or screenshot

Any image, such as a screenshot from a computer game or instant messaging text discussion, requires the *who, what, where,* and *when* information. If the screenshot or image has no title, you may need to give the source a title to help the reader understand and locate the source if possible.

> Associated Press. *Cassius Clay Malcolm X.* 1964. AP Images, www.apimages .com/metadata/Index/Associated-Press-Domestic-News-New-York-United -/62c2ee253ae5da11af9f0014c2589dfb/15/1.

Audio, Video, and Broadcast Sources

21. Television or radio

Television and radio broadcasts use the same sequence of information; however, the *where* information is the title of the program or series, such as *Nightly News with Lester Holt*, the name of the broadcasting network, such as NBC, and the call letters of the broadcasting station, such as WMAQ Chicago.

> "La Mancha Screwjob." *Radiolab*, narrated by Jad Abumrad and Robert
> Krulwich, National Public Radio, KBSX, Boise, 24 Dec. 2017.

22. Sound recording

A published sound recording is often the product of a number of artists, such as lead soloist, ensemble, composer, and conductor. Often, the name you discovered during the research that led you to the sound recording should be the same name you use to begin your citation. Your citation should begin with the name you use in your argument or the name used in the parenthetical citation.

A. Recording in physical format

> Adler, Richard, and Jerry Ross. *Damn Yankees: Original Broadway Cast
> Recording.* Performances by Gwen Verdon, Stephen Douglass, and Ray
> Walston, directed by Hal Hastings, BMG Music, 1988.

B. Recording downloaded

> Wilco. "Random Name Generator." *Star Wars*, by Jeff Tweedy, dBpm
> Records, 2015, wilcoworld.net/music/star-wars/.

23. Lecture or performance

A live lecture or a play, dance, or other performance will be cited in a similar way. The primary difference is that citations for performances typically begin with the title of the work performed.

A. Lecture or reading

> Lythcott-Haims, Julie. "How to Raise an Adult." 92nd Street Y, 16 July 2015,
> New York.

B. Performance

> Shakespeare, William. *Hamlet*. Directed by Austin Pendleton, performance
> by Peter Sarsgaard, Classic Stage Company, 27 Mar. 2015, New York.

Online Sources

24. Website

Websites can be a challenge to document simply because there is no standard place to find publication information, as there is on the title and copyright pages of a book, for example. Still, answers to the *who*, *what*, *where*, and *when* questions should be available at the bottom of the home page or on the "About Us" page. Because websites are revised and change often, provide your reader with the date when you accessed the source, unless the citation is for a dated entry such as a blog post.

> CERN. (2017, September 29). *ATLAS releases first result using full
> LHC Run 2 dataset*. https://home.cern/news/news/physics/
> atlas-releases-first-result-using-full-lhc-run-2-dataset

25. Wiki entry

There are many types of wikis, including some built by enthusiasts who are not experts and some that are built by and for experts and scholars to share information. Because wikis are developed collaboratively, authors' names are rarely cited. Obviously, you should examine any wiki carefully to determine its authority before using it as a source.

> "Mammalian Bites." *WikEM, The Global Emergency Medicine Wiki*, OpenEM
> Foundation, 15 June 2015, wikem.org/wiki/Mammalian_bites.

26. Social network

> Savage, Doug. "How to Train Your Cat." *Facebook*, 2 Feb. 2017,
> www.facebook.com/savage.chickens.

A tweet is so brief that the entire tweet is used as the *what* information. The container is identified as "*Twitter*," and the local time when the message was sent is enough information for the reader to locate this type of source.

Department of Defense [@DeptofDefense]. "From 1 SecDef to another: Hagel
   calls @timhowardgk to say thanks for defending USA. We (USA) are
   proud of @ussoccer!" *Twitter*, 2 July 2014, twitter.com/deptofdefense/
   status/484438026152460288.

27. News group, discussion board, blog

Kiko, Jennifer. "Night Light." *Farmgirl Follies*, 9 July 2015,
   www.farmgirlfollies.com/2015/07/night-light-20024.html.

28. Email

Peters, K.J. "Re: Avoid the Turtles." E-mail to Alex Neel, 25 Dec. 2017.

29. Online video and audio

A. Streamed movie or TV

Movies and television shows may have several creators and contributors. You should
begin your citation with the name of the individual that is the focus of your discussion, and the reason you are using the source. For example, if you want to examine
the editing of a movie, begin with the name of the editor. If you are examining an
actor's performance in a television show, begin with that actor's name. You are free
to add other significant contributors if it will help the audience locate the source.

Bathurst, Otto, director. "National Anthem." *Black Mirror*, season 1, episode
   1, 4 Dec. 2011. *Netflix*, www.netflix.com/title/70264888.

B. YouTube video

An online video must cite the website, such as YouTube, as the container and identify
the uploader as another contributor. However, you do not need to repeat the name
of the uploader if they are also the creator.

Film Theorists. "Harry Potter, More Voldemort Than Voldemort!" *YouTube*,
   17 Jan. 2017, www.youtube.com/watch?v=mbC-sDMHypU.

C. Podcasts

Abumrad, Jade. "Stranger in Paradise." *Radiolab*, 27 Jan. 2017, www.radio
   lab.org/story/stanger-paradise/.

Other Digital Sources

30. PDF

Ramist, Leonard, Charles Lewis, and Laura McCamley. "Student Group Differences in Predicting College Grades: Sex, Language, and Ethnic Groups." *ETS Research Report Series*, vol. 1994, no. 1, 1994, pp. 1–41, research.collegeboard.org/sites /default/files/publications/2012/7/researchreport-1993-1-student-group-differences-predicting-college-grades.pdf. File last modified on 8 Aug. 2014.

31. DVD or film

"Christmas at Downton Abbey." *Downton Abbey*, written by Julian Fellowes, directed by Brian Percival, season 2, episode 9, PBS, 2012, disc 3. DVD.

The Great Gatsby. Directed by Baz Luhrmann, performances by Leonardo DiCaprio, Tobey Maguire, Carey Mulligan, and Joel Edgerton, Warner Bros., 2013.

32. An app

The citation of computer software or apps is very similar to online or downloaded books. Apps have titles, containers such as Microsoft Teams or the Apple App Store, publishers, and dates of publication. The author can be the creator or the copyright holder of the app.

Aspyr Media. *Sim City: Complete Edition*. Version 1.0.2, Aspyr Media, Inc., 30 Mar. 2015, Apple App Store.

Excerpts from a Student Paper in MLA Style

The MLA style includes formatting expectations for margins, line spacing, and captions. The first page and works-cited page from a paper formatted in MLA style are presented below.

Adonis Williams wrote the paper for his Irish literature course, in which the professor expected students to use MLA style.

This is the order of identifying info that MLA recommends, but your professor may have a different preference.

Use a common font like Arial or Times New Roman. Use 12 point font size and double-spacing.

One inch margins top, both sides, and bottom.

The last name and page number appear on every page, top right.

The MLA does not require title pages, though if your professor asks for one, follow the format he or she recommends.

Number and name all images as "Fig." Also, refer to figures within the text.

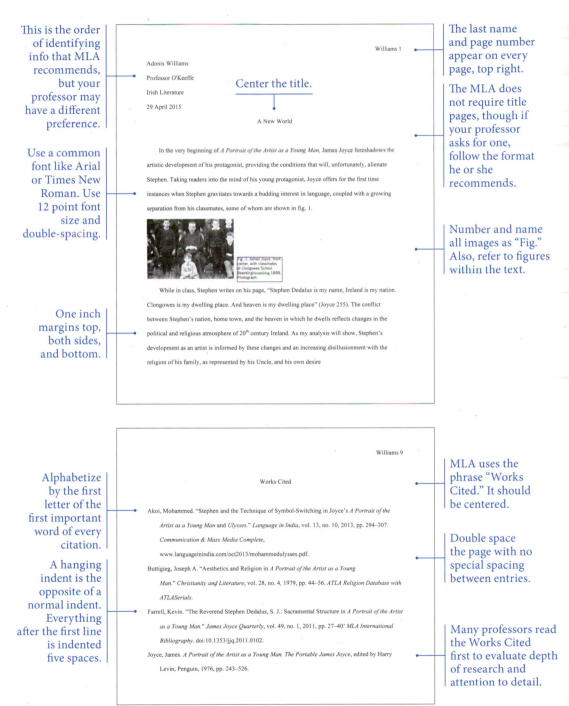

Williams 1

Adonis Williams

Professor O'Keeffe

Irish Literature

29 April 2015

Center the title.

A New World

In the very beginning of *A Portrait of the Artist as a Young Man*, James Joyce foreshadows the artistic development of his protagonist, providing the conditions that will, unfortunately, alienate Stephen. Taking readers into the mind of his young protagonist, Joyce offers for the first time instances when Stephen gravitates towards a budding interest in language, coupled with a growing separation from his classmates, some of whom are shown in fig. 1.

Fig. 1. James Joyce, front center, with classmates at Clongowes School. Boardinghouseblog 1888. Photograph.

While in class, Stephen writes on his page, "Stephen Dedalus is my name, Ireland is my nation. Clongowes is my dwelling place. And heaven is my dwelling place" (Joyce 255). The conflict between Stephen's nation, home town, and the heaven in which he dwells reflects changes in the political and religious atmosphere of 20th century Ireland. As my analysis will show, Stephen's development as an artist is informed by these changes and an increasing disillusionment with the religion of his family, as represented by his Uncle, and his own desire

Alphabetize by the first letter of the first important word of every citation.

A hanging indent is the opposite of a normal indent. Everything after the first line is indented five spaces.

MLA uses the phrase "Works Cited." It should be centered.

Double space the page with no special spacing between entries.

Many professors read the Works Cited first to evaluate depth of research and attention to detail.

Williams 9

Works Cited

Akoi, Mohammed. "Stephen and the Technique of Symbol-Switching in Joyce's *A Portrait of the Artist as a Young Man* and *Ulysses.*" *Language in India*, vol. 13, no. 10, 2013, pp. 294–307. *Communication & Mass Media Complete*, www.languageinindia.com/oct2013/mohammedulysses.pdf.

Buttigieg, Joseph A. "Aesthetics and Religion in *A Portrait of the Artist as a Young Man.*" *Christianity and Literature*, vol. 28, no. 4, 1979, pp. 44–56. *ATLA Religion Database with ATLASerials*.

Farrell, Kevin. "The Reverend Stephen Dedalus, S. J.: Sacramental Structure in *A Portrait of the Artist as a Young Man.*" *James Joyce Quarterly*, vol. 49, no. 1, 2011, pp. 27–40. *MLA International Bibliography*. doi:10.1353/jjq.2011.0102.

Joyce, James. *A Portrait of the Artist as a Young Man. The Portable James Joyce*, edited by Harry Levin, Penguin, 1976, pp. 243–526.

MODULE VII-3

APA STYLE FOR IN-TEXT CITATIONS

The documentation style recommended by the American Psychological Association, or the **APA style**, is used by disciplines in the social sciences such as psychology, linguistics, economics, and political science. The following guidelines are based on the 7th edition of the *Publication Manual of the American Psychological Association* (2020).

As with any documentation style, the purpose of the APA style is to give your reader the information necessary to link a source you use in your argument to the original source as efficiently as possible. The APA style is composed of brief citations in the text of your argument that point to the list of references with full bibliographic information at the end.

In-text citations have three parts: the family name of the author, the year of publication, and for quotations and specific information the page number. In-text citations appear in the body of an essay, immediately after or before material from a source that has been integrated into the text.

The list of **references** is arranged in alphabetical order at the end of the text. Each entry provides the answers to the *who, what, when,* and *where* information needed to find a source using any library, search engine, or database (Figure 7.2).

Unlike Freud and those who followed in his footsteps, Laing (2010) was not interested in theoretically bound diagnoses, but was more focused upon understanding the experience of insanity and helping the common reader understand distressed states of mind, as in the case of Peter (pp. 120-133).

References

Laing, R. D. (2010). *The divided self: An existential study in sanity and madness.* Penguin UK.

The date of publication always follows the author's name in the text. When citing quotations, summaries or paraphrases of specific ideas in a work, include page numbers.

Figure 7.2
An in-text citation, and a reference entry, for a book by R.D. Laing.

In-Text Citations Focus on Who, When, and Where

In-text citations answer *who* (the author or authors), *when* (the year a work was published), and, for quotations and specific information, a small part of *where* (page numbers where the quotation can be found within a source).

Identifying an author in an integrating phrase or sentence is the method that writing instructors and other professors generally prefer and is a more effective way to incorporate information from a source than placing all the information in a parenthetical citation. When identifying the author or authors of a work for the first time, use each author's family name only.

Date of publication is of special importance to all types of scientists, including those in the social sciences. In fact, the APA calls its method of in-text citation "the author-date method." The sciences progress quickly, and recent discoveries and recent revisions of findings and theories drive these disciplines forward. As a result, a student or researcher who is aware of the most recent peer-reviewed research coming out of the Large Hadron Collider speaks with greater authority than someone citing data from the Relativistic Heavy Ion Collider, which was a predecessor to the Hadron Collider and seems like an antique now. Therefore, in-text citations always include the year of publication in parentheses.

Page numbers, when available, are a useful tool for locating cited sources. In APA style, page numbers are required for quotations and specific information. Many contemporary sources do not use page numbers, however. The following practices will help you deal with page numbers:

- If you are referring to an entire book or summarizing an entire work, page numbers are not necessary in the in-text citation.
- If you can find page numbers, use them in the parenthetical reference.
- Place a comma after the year if you are including a page number, and use "p." as an abbreviation for "page" or "pp." for "pages."
- If paragraph numbers are available instead of page numbers, use "para." as the abbreviation for "paragraph."
- If there are no page or paragraph numbers, use the first few distinctive words of a heading within quotation marks, followed by the number of the paragraph in which the quotation appears: "Final Thoughts," para. 3. If the heading is too long, abbreviate it.
- If none of the above is available, the date within parentheses is sufficient.

Example In-Text Citations

1. One author identified in an integrating sentence
When you introduce the author of a source in the sentence that includes the parentheses, there is no need to repeat his or her name in parentheses. The year and, if needed, the page number, are sufficient.

> Laing (2010) was focused upon understanding the experience of going insane and helping the common reader understand distressed states of mind.

A direct quotation of an author's specific idea requires a page number. A summary or paraphrase of an author's ideas does not require page numbers according to the APA; however, you may provide page numbers if you think it will help your reader or affirm your authority.

> Cather's (1918) sense of the lives of Nebraska farmers and the power of the land is captured by the narrator of *My Ántonia* when he thinks, "At any rate, that is happiness; to be dissolved into something complete and great" (p. 14).

2. One author in a parenthetical citation
Note that a comma separates the author from the year of publication.

> Unlike Freud and those who followed in his footsteps, other therapists were more focused upon understanding the experience of insanity (Laing, 2010).

3. Two authors identified in an integrating sentence
Cite the names of both authors each time you refer to their work.

> Watson and Crick's (1953) article "A structure for deoxyribose nucleic acid" is renowned for first describing DNA as we know it today, but it should also be celebrated for doing so in 15 brief paragraphs.

4. Two authors in a parenthetical citation
If you do not identify the author or authors in the integrating sentence, use the family name of each in parentheses, separated by an ampersand (&).

> The essay that first described DNA as we know it today (Watson & Crick, 1953) is only 15 paragraphs long.

5. Three or more authors identified in an integrating sentence

When you use a source with three or more authors include only the family name of the first author followed by "et al." The abbreviation "et al." always includes a period.

> There is no doubt designers and programmers can resolve the uncanny valley. However, it should be noted that Saygin et al. (2011) end their study by suggesting we may not want robots to look anything like us (p. 420).

6. Three or more authors in a parenthetical citation

Similarly, for three or more authors in a parenthetical citation, include only the first author's family name and "et al."

> Not surprisingly, cognitive research confirms Freud's theory of the "uncanny" (Saygin et al., 2011, p. 420).

7. Group author identified in an integrating sentence

For the citation of a source produced by a group such as a corporation or organization, the group's name is included in full in the text. If the name is long, it may be abbreviated after the first use of the source.

> The US Dry Bean Council (2015) argues that it is almost impossible to meet the USDA's inspection standards for "insect webs and filth."

8. Group author in a parenthetical citation

If a group has authored your source, use the full name of the group in the first parenthetical citation.

> The President's Executive Order 12333 prevents the US government and its agencies from using satellites and other methods of intelligence collection against US citizens on US soil (National Geospatial-Intelligence Agency).

In subsequent references to the same source, you may use the first few distinctive words of long group names.

> US citizens overseas may be subject to the collection of intelligence information by way of satellite-based communication or observation monitoring (National Geospatial).

9. Anonymous author in an integrating sentence

If the information about who authored a document, text, or work is not available, the *what*—that is, the title—is the means of identifying the source and connecting it to the list of references. The first time you use a source in your argument, state the full title. Thereafter you may use the first few distinct words of a title if it is long.

> In "One More Punch" (2015), we are reminded that Ivermectin has been around since the 1980s (p. 76).

10. Anonymous author in a parenthetical citation

If a source lists an author as "anonymous," use the same word in the parenthetical citation.

> Of course, identity is never a sure thing (Anonymous, 1912, p. 238).

If there is no indication of an author, use the title of the work in the parenthetical citation. If the title is long, use the first few distinct words of the title.

> The coywolf, half coyote and half wolf, numbers in the millions ("Evolution: Greater Than," 2015).

11. Personal communication

Emails and other personal communication such as interviews, memos, letters, and conversations are cited in the text but are not included in the list of references. Since these citations do not provide information that would help a reader locate the original, APA considers it unnecessary to include them in the list of references. Identify the person you spoke with by initials and include the date.

> D. Ryan was insistent that this is Everton's century (personal communication, April 14, 2015).

> This is Everton's century (D. Ryan, personal communication, April 14, 2015).

MODULE VII-4

APA LIST OF REFERENCES

In the APA style, the references list at the end of your argument includes a single entry for each source you cite within the text. Each entry provides detailed answers to the *who*, *what*, *when*, and *where* questions, allowing the reader to locate the exact source you used.

Elements of Style for References Citations

References page format. The references page begins with the word "References" as the centered title. Double space each citation, and alphabetize each entry using the first word of the in-text citation (name, group, or title).

Sequence. In the APA style, the answers to *who*, *what*, *when*, and *where* are consistently in the same order, with few exceptions. APA style includes information such as a digital object identifier, or DOI, or the uniform resource locator, or URL, for documents retrieved or available from online sources. Pages numbers always include all digits.

Author   Date Published   Title   Publisher

Kerouac, J. (1962). *Big Sur*. Penguin.

Hanging indent. A hanging indent is the reverse of a normal indent. The first line begins at the margin and all following lines of the same entry are indented one-half inch or five spaces.

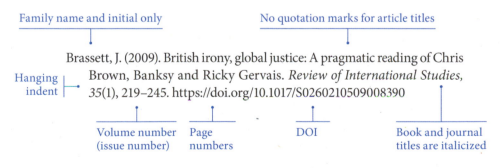

Family name and initial only   No quotation marks for article titles

Brassett, J. (2009). British irony, global justice: A pragmatic reading of Chris Brown, Banksy and Ricky Gervais. *Review of International Studies,* 35(1), 219–245. https://doi.org/10.1017/S0260210509008390

Hanging indent

Volume number   Page   DOI   Book and journal
(issue number)   numbers   titles are italicized

The references are alphabetized by the family name, group name, or the first important word of the title that starts the citation.

Capitalization rules for journals are not the same as the rules for other sources. All significant words in journal titles are capitalized. However, only the first word of a book title, book chapter title, or website is capitalized, along with the first word after a colon.

The **author, authors, authoring group, or title** leads the citation. If there is an author, the *who* information in the citation must connect to the name or names that appear in the text, either in the integrating sentence or in parentheses. The APA lists names, groups, and titles in the same way for all types of documents, texts, and works.

Example References Citations for Different Types of Authorship

1. One author
Use the author's family name followed by the first initial of the first name and middle name, if any.

> Cather, W. (2009). *My Ántonia*. Oxford University Press.

2. Two authors

> Cook, P. J., & Goss, K. A. (2014). *The gun debate: What everyone needs to know.* Oxford University Press.

3. Three to twenty authors
For all authors, use the family name followed by first initial of the first name and middle name if any, and separate all names with a comma. Prior to the last name, use "&" in place of "and."

> Saygin, A. P., Chaminade, T., Ishiguro, H., Driver, J., & Frith, C. (2012). The thing that should not be: Predictive coding and the uncanny valley in perceiving human and humanoid robot actions. *Social Cognitive and Affective Neuroscience, 7*(4), 413–422. https://doi:10.1093/scan/nsr025

4. More than twenty authors
List the first nineteen authors, then use three ellipses to indicate names missing, and then add the last of the author's names.

> Aad, G., Abajyan, T., Abbott, B., Abdallah, J., Abdel Khalek, S., Abdelalim, A. A., Abdinov, O., Aben, R., Abi, B., Abolins, M., AbouZeid, O. S., Abramowicz, H., Abreu, H., Acharya, B. S., Adamczyk, L., Adams, D.

L., Addy, T. N., Adelman, J., Adomeit, S., Zwalinski, L (2012). Observation of a new particle in the search for the Standard Model Higgs boson with the ATLAS detector at the LHC. *Physics Letters B, 716*(1), 1–29. https://doi:10.1016/j.physletb.2012.08.020

5. A group, organization, or corporate author

Government documents and reports put out by corporations and other groups often list a group name, such as the Rand Corporation or the National Geospatial-Intelligence Agency, as the author. In such cases, the full name of the group is used and alphabetized based on the first important word in the name (not *a*, *an*, or *the*).

National Research Council: Committee on the Biological Effects of Ionizing Radiations, & United States. (1980). *The effects on populations of exposure to low levels of ionizing radiation, 1980* (vol. 3095). National Academy Press.

6. Anonymous documents, texts, and works

If no author of any kind is identified by the source, move the title, or *what* information, to the beginning of the citation.

One more punch. (2015, October 31). *The Economist, 417*(8962), 76.

7. Two or more documents, texts, or works by the same author

If you are citing two or more books by the same author, list the earliest publication date first.

Kerouac, J. (1962). *Big Sur.* Penguin.

Kerouac, J. (2007). *On the road: The original scroll.* Penguin.

If you are citing one work by a single author and another work where the author was the lead author of a work with multiple authors, the single-author citation should come first.

Saygin, A. P. (2007). Superior temporal and premotor brain areas necessary for biological motion perception. *Brain, 130*(9), 2452–2461.

Saygin, A. P., Chaminade, T., Ishiguro, H., Driver, J., & Frith, C. (2012). The thing that should not be: Predictive coding and the uncanny valley in perceiving human and humanoid robot actions. *Social Cognitive and Affective Neuroscience, 7*(4), 413–422. https://doi:10.1093/scan/nsr025

Responsible Sourcing
APA Abbreviations

The APA, like many style manuals and handbooks, uses its own set of abbreviations. The following are used in references.

doi:—digital object identifier
ed.—edition
Ed.—Editor
n.d.—no date
n.p.—no place
n.p.—no publisher
n. pag.—no page
No.—number
p.—page
pp.—pages
Pt.—Part
Trans.—Translator
Vol.—volume

Example Reference Citations for Different Types of Sources

The listing of author's or authoring group's names is the same no matter what kind of source is being documented. And the sequence of the *who*, *what*, *when*, and *where* information will also be consistent. However, the *where* information may include different types of information, such as a DOI number or URL.

Make sure you have one reference citation for each source you use in the text of your argument. Always cite the same version of a source you consulted when you did your research. Books or articles with the same author and title can differ from each other in terms of editing and page numbers. For example, the Knopf edition of Toni Morrison's *The Bluest Eye* is 215 pages long, but the Vintage reprint is 224 pages long. In addition, different editors working with the same text can make different edits, cuts, and revisions.

Below, you will find documentation models for the following broad types of sources:

- books
- periodicals or sources published regularly
- visuals

- broadcast, audio, and video sources
- online sources
- other digital sources

Books

1. Print or digital book

A. The **print** citation sets the pattern for all book citations.

> Kerouac, J. (1962). *Big Sur*. Penguin.

B. For an **electronic book** that has content different from the print version, indicate the electronic version and add the URL.

> Kerouac, J. (2012). *Big Sur* [Kindle edition]. Penguin. https://www.amazon.com/gp/product/B00601W8L2?tag=randohouseinc7986-20

2. An introduction, foreword, or afterword of a book

Begin the citation with the name of the person who wrote the introduction, foreword, or afterword. Use the title or word that best describes your source, such as "Introduction" or "Foreword."

> Slethaug, G. E. (2014). Introduction. In *Adaptation theory and criticism: Postmodern literature and cinema in the USA* (pp. 1–12). Bloomsbury.

If the author of the introduction, foreword, or afterword is different from the author of the book, the author of the work being cited begins the citation. The name of the book author appears after "In."

> Sharistanian, J. (2008). Introduction. In W. Cather *My Ántonia* (pp. vii–xxiv). Oxford University Press.

3. A selection or part of a book or anthology

For any selection that appears within another book, such as an essay or a short story in an anthology, remember the larger book or anthology is where the selection is located. The citation begins with the author of the selection, followed by the title of the selection, with no quotation marks. The title of the book or anthology is italicized and the page numbers are in parentheses.

Derrida, J. (1995). Between brackets (P. Kamuf, Trans.). In W. Hamacher & D. Wellbery (Eds.), *Points…: Interviews, 1974–1994* (pp. 5–29). Stanford University Press.

4. Book with an editor or translator

The names of an editor or a translator are placed in parentheses and follow the title. For an editor use "Ed." and for a translator use "Trans."

Kolmogorov, A. (1950). *Foundations of the theory of probability* (N. Morrison, Ed. & Trans.). Chelsea.

5. Book with a volume or an edition number

A. A book with a volume number is one of a set of books that have the same title. The volume number is part of the title. Use "Vol." for "Volume."

Freud, S. (2001). *The standard edition of the complete psychological works of Sigmund Freud* (Vol. 7, J. Strachey, Ed.). Vintage.

B. An edition is a version of a book or one of many printings of a book. Place the edition number in parentheses following the title and use "ed." for "edition."

Meier, P., & Zünd, R. (2000). *Statistics for analytical chemistry* (2nd ed.). Wiley.

Periodicals or Sources Published Regularly

6. An article in a scholarly journal

Articles in scholarly journals are written for and read by experts, scholars, professors, or others who seek information about current research in a specific discipline. Journals can be published monthly, every six months, or once a year, for example. As a result, citations for articles in scholarly journals provide more specific *where* information by including the volume number and issue number in addition to page numbers.

Citations for both print articles and those published electronically should include the DOI (digital object identifier) if one is available. A DOI is a specific code that provides an enduring link to a work that will not change or get lost. DOIs will be found on the first page of an electronically published article, next to the copyright notice, or on the web page that contains the article. If a DOI number is not available, use the URL (uniform resource locator). The DOI or URL is not followed by a period.

A. An article from a **print scholarly journal**

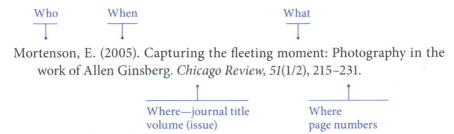

Mortenson, E. (2005). Capturing the fleeting moment: Photography in the work of Allen Ginsberg. *Chicago Review, 51*(1/2), 215–231.

B. An article from an **online scholarly journal** is cited like a print article

Maia, C., Aparecido, J., & Milanez, L. (2004). Thermally developing forced convection of non-Newtonian fluids inside elliptical ducts. *Heat Transfer Engineering, 25*(7), 13–22. https://doi:10.1080/01457630490495805

Lippit, A. M. (2011). David Lynch's wholes. *Flow, 15*(3). http://www.flowjournal.org/2011/11/david-lynchs-wholes/

C. An article from an **online database** is cited slightly differently than an online journal. There is no need to identify the database name, such as EBSCO or JSTOR. However, the database name can be provided if it adds useful information such as context. The DOI number is preferred, but if one is not available use the URL.

Grahn, H., von Schoenberg, P., & Brännström, N. (2015 March 18). Who farted? Hydrogen sulphide transport from Bardarbunga to Scandinavia. *arXiv preprint*. https://doi:arXiv:1503.05327

7. Magazines

Magazine citations are similar to scholarly journal citations. However, because magazines may be published monthly or weekly, the citation needs to include the specific month or day of publication.

A. An article in a magazine published monthly

Mathews, D. (2014, December/2015, January). It's Austin Mahone's world and we're all just living in it. *TeenVogue*, 53–56.

B. An article in a magazine published weekly

Foroohar, R. (2015, February 5). Starbucks for America. *Time, 185*(5), 23–27.

C. An online magazine article

Griswold, A. (2015, March 23). The world's taxi unions may have just convinced the U.N. to stop working with Uber. *Slate*. https://slate.com/
business/2015/03/u-n-women-cancels-partnership-with-uber-a-rift-over-
creating-1-million-jobs-by-2020.html

8. Newspaper

An article in a newspaper must indicate the page and section number of the newspaper, if they are available.

A. An article in a newspaper

Musetto, V. (1983, April 15). Headless body in topless bar. *New York Post*, p. A1.

B. An article from a newspaper online edition

Rocha, V. (2015, February 9). Arrest made in death of transgender woman after
O.C. silicone party. *Los Angeles Times*. https://www.latimes.com/local/
lanow/la-me-ln-transgender-silicone-party-death-20150209-story.html

C. A review of a book or other type of work

If the author and book reviewed are not named in the title of the review, use "Review
of" and name the title and author in brackets following the title.

Cisneros, S. (2015, October 18). Sandra Cisneros' 6 favorite restorative books
[Review of *Teresita*, by W. C. Holden]. *The Week*. https://theweek.com/
articles/583335/sandra-cisneros-6-favorite-restorative-books

King, S. (2013, October 10). Flights of fancy: Donna Tartt's *Goldfinch*. *The
New York Times Book Review*, p. 1.

Government-Sponsored or Related Document

9. Government documents

Government documents and government-sponsored documents may list only the
government or specific agency as the author. Also, it is possible that the publisher
is the same as the author.

A. A printed government document

Presidential Commission on the Space Shuttle Challenger Accident. (1986). *Report to the President.* 5 vols. (GPO Publication No. 62-885 0). Government Printing Office.

B. A government document published online

Many government agencies issue reports by the same name periodically. After the title of the work, state the report number or date of issuance in parentheses to help identify which report you are citing.

Office of Naval Intelligence. (2008, April 23). *World wide threat to shipping (WTS) report.* http://msi.nga.mil/MSISiteContent/StaticFiles/MISC/wwtts/wwtts_20080423100000.txt

Office of Naval Intelligence. (2017, February 1). *World wide threat to shipping (WTS) report.* http://msi.nga.mil/MSISiteContent/StaticFiles/MISC/wwtts/wwtts_20170202100000.txt

Interviews

Interviews appear in almost any genre or format and may also be unpublished, as in a phone interview. APA interview citations follow the referencing style for the format in which they appear. If you conducted the interview yourself, cite the interview in the text but do not include an entry in the list of references (see p. 204).

10. Interviews

A. A printed interview

Nancy, J. (1991). "Eating well," or the calculation of the subject: An interview with Jacques Derrida. In In E. Cadava, P. Connor, & J-L Nancy (Eds.), *Who comes after the subject?* Routledge.

B. Interview from an online source

Widmer, T. (2010, summer). R. Crumb, The art of comics no. 1. *The Paris Review, 193.* https://www.theparisreview.org/interviews/6017/the-art-of-comics-no-1-r-crumb

Visuals

11. Map or chart

Maps are commonly part of a book or atlas, such as in example A below. They can also be available as individual sheets. A map citation provides the name of the creator, or cartographer, and the name of the map in the usual sequence. If no name is provided, give the map a title that would make it easy to identify and fits the context in which it was found. In addition, include a brief description of the type of map or chart in brackets following the map title.

A. Print map

> Paullin, C. (1975). Settled area 1760 and population 1750 [Demographic map]. In J. Wright (Ed.), *Atlas of the historical geography of the United States* (p. 60). Greenwood Press.

B. Downloaded chart

> Federal Aviation Administration. (2015). Omaha SEC 92. *Sectional raster aeronautical chart.* http://www.faa.gov/air_traffic/flight_info/aeronav/digital_products/vfr/

12. Image or screenshot

Any screenshot, such as an image from a computer game or instant messaging text discussion, requires the *who*, *what*, *when*, and *where* information. You may need to give the source a descriptive title and in brackets provide a brief description of the format.

> *Cassius Clay Malcolm X* [Photograph]. (1 Mar. 1964). AP Images. www.apimages.com/metadata/Index/Associated-Press-Domestic-News-New-York-United-/62c2ee253ae5da11af9f0014c2589dfb/15/1

Broadcast, Audio, and Video Sources

13. Television or radio broadcast or podcast

Television and radio broadcasts are similar to a citation for a selection from a book. Begin the citation with the scriptwriter and director as the *who* information, if available. Producers can be listed in the same way as editors.

Abumrad, J. (Producer). (2015, February 24). La Mancha screwjob [Audio podcast episode]. In *Radiolab*. WNYC Studios. https://www.wnyc.org/radio/#/ondemand/433231

14. Sound recording

A published sound recording is often the product of a number of creators, such as lead soloist, ensemble, composer, and conductor. Your citation should begin with the name you cite in your argument. List the manner of each artist's contribution in parentheses. Often, the name you discovered during the research that led you to the sound recording should be the same name you use to begin your citation.

A. Recording in physical format

Adler, R. (Writer and Composer), & Ross, J. (Composer and Lyricist). (1988). *Damn Yankees: Original Broadway cast recording* [CD]. BMG Music.

B. Song

Wilco. (2015). Random name generator [Song]. On *Star Wars* [Album]. dBpm Records. http://wilcoworld.net/splash-star-wars-links/

Online Sources

15. Website

Websites can be a challenge to document simply because there is no standard place to find publication information, as there is on the title and copyright pages of a book, for example. Still, answers to the *who*, *what*, *when*, and *where* questions should be available at the bottom of the home page or on the "About Us" page. If not, you can use the APA abbreviations (see box above, p. 208) to indicate the missing information.

A. A selection from a website

"ATLAS Releases First Result Using Full LHC Run 2 Dataset." *CERN*, 29 Sept. 2017, https://home.cern/news/news/physics/atlas-releases-first-result-using-full-lhc-run-2-dataset. Accessed 14 Feb. 2019.

B. Wiki entry

There are many types of wikis, including some built by enthusiasts who are not experts and some that are built by and for experts and scholars to share information. Because wikis are developed collaboratively, authors of entries are rarely cited. Obviously, you should evaluate a wiki in terms of its authority before citing it in an argument.

> *Mammalian bites*. (n.d.). WikEM, the global emergency medicine wiki. Retrieved March 20, 2017, from https://www.wikem.org/wiki/ Mammalian_bites

C. Social network post

> Savage, D. (2017, February 2). *How to train your cat* [Image attached] [Status update]. Facebook. www.facebook.com/savage.chickens

A tweet is so brief that the entire tweet may be used as the *what* information. Provide the content or caption of the post (up to the first 20 words) as the title. The format is identified as "Tweet" in brackets.

> Department of Defense [@DeptofDefense]. (2014, July 2). *From 1 SecDef to another: Hagel calls @timhowardgk to say thanks for defending USA. We (USA) are proud of @ussoccer!* [Tweet]. Twitter. https://twitter.com/ deptofdefense/status/484438026152460288

D. Newsgroup, discussion board, blog

> Kiko, J. (2015, September 23). Night light. *Farm Girl Follies*. http://www. farmgirlfollies.com/2015/07/night-light-20024.html

16. Online video and audio

A. Streamed movie or TV

Movies and television shows may have several creators and contributors. In APA style, you begin your citation with the name of the most immediate creator of the work you are citing. For example, if you are citing an entire series of streamed episodes, you would begin your citation with the name of the producer. If you are citing a specific episode, cite the writer and director first, and then include the name of the producer after the title.

> Brooker, C. (Writer), & Bathurst, O. (Director). (2011, December 4). National Anthem (Season 1, Episode 1) [V series episode]. In *Black Mirror*. Netflix. http://www.netflix.com/title/70264888

B. YouTube video

A YouTube video citation begins with the creator's name, typically the username, followed by the date uploaded, name of the video, and a description of the source in brackets.

> Film Theorists. (2017). *Harry Potter, more Voldemort than Voldemort!* [Video]. YouTube. https://www.youtube.com/watch?v=mbC-sDMHypU

C. Podcasts

> Lechtenberg, S. (Executive Producer). (2002-present). *Radiolab* [Audio podcast]. WNYC Studios. https://www.wnycstudios.org/podcasts/radiolab

Other Digital Sources

17. PDF

> Ramist, L., Lewis, C., & McCamley, L. (1994). Student group differences in predicting college grades: Sex, language, and ethnic groups. *ETS Research Report Series*, *1994*(1), pp. 1–41. https://research.collegeboard.org/sites/default/files/publications/2012/7/researchreport-1993-1-student-group-differences-predicting-college-grades.pdf

18. DVD or film

> Fellowes, J. (Writer), & Percival, B. (Director). (2012). Christmas at Downton Abbey (Season 2, Episode 9) [V series episode]. In J. Fellowes & G. Neames (Producers), *Downton Abbey: Season 2* [DVD]. PBS.

> Luhrmann, B. (Director). (2013). *The Great Gatsby* [Film]. Warner Bros.

Excerpts from a Student Paper in APA Style

APA style includes formatting expectations for margins, line spacing, and captions. The first page and References page from a paper formatted in APA style are presented below. Hannah Gioia wrote the following paper for her First Year Seminar.

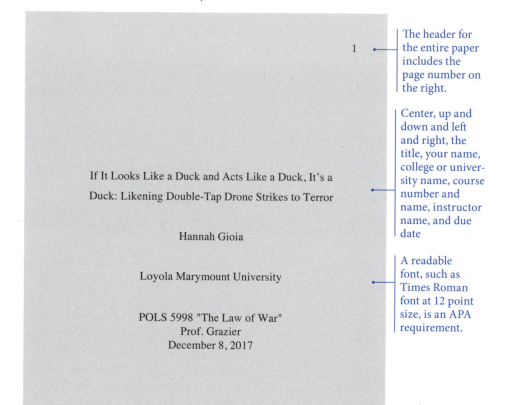

1

If It Looks Like a Duck and Acts Like a Duck, It's a

Duck: Likening Double-Tap Drone Strikes to Terror

Hannah Gioia

Loyola Marymount University

POLS 5998 "The Law of War"
Prof. Grazier
December 8, 2017

The header for the entire paper includes the page number on the right.

Center, up and down and left and right, the title, your name, college or university name, course number and name, instructor name, and due date

A readable font, such as Times Roman font at 12 point size, is an APA requirement.

2

If It Looks Like a Duck and Acts Like a Duck, It's a Duck: Likening
Double-Tap Drone Strikes to Terror Tactics

Are U.S. double-tap drone strikes a form of terrorism? The first
obvious obstacle to answering this question is the lack of consensus
among scholars, states, and international organizations as to what, exactly,
terrorism is in a definitional sense. While this paper does not attempt to
discern the elusive definition of terrorism, it will adopt common criteria
found in many pre-existing, scholarly definitions and
test double-tap drone strikes against those sets of standards. The second
obstacle to addressing this question is the disagreement among scholars of
whether or not "state terrorism" is even a legitimate distinction to make
since non-state terrorism is a more accepted field of study.

The idea that states cannot, themselves, commit acts of terror can be
traced back to Max Weber's claim that states enjoy "the monopoly of the
legitimate use of physical force within a given territory" (Weber, 1965).
Countries have a vested interest in maintaining the idea that they enjoy a
certain legitimacy, a privilege of power, when it comes to the use of
violence, intrastate or interstate. For example, the U.S. Department of
State defines terrorism as "politically motivated violence perpetrated
against noncombatant targets by subnational groups or clandestine agents,
usually intended to influence an audience" (U.S. Code). Noticeably
missing is the possibility of a state actor committing an act of terror.
They, the states, benefit from distancing their forms of violence from the

Center
the title.

One inch
margins at
the top, both
sides, and
bottom.

The References list always starts a new page.

14

References

Armborst, A. (2010). Modelling terrorism and political violence. *International Relations*, *24*(4), 414–432. https://doi.org/10.1177%2F0047117810385779

Broomhall, B. (2004). State actors in an international definition of terrorism from a human rights perspective. *Case Western Reserve Journal of International Law*, *36*, 421. https://scholarlycommons.law.case.edu/jil/vol36/iss2/9

Crenshaw, M. (1987). Theories of terrorism: Instrumental and organizational approaches. *Journal of Strategic Studies*, *10*(4), 13–31. https://doi.org/10.1080/01402398708437313

Friedrichs, J. (2006). Defining the international public enemy: The political struggle behind the legal debate on international terrorism. *Leiden Journal of International Law*, *19*(1), 69. https://doi.org/10.1017/S0922156505003183

Ganor, B. (2002). Defining terrorism: Is one man's terrorist another man's freedom fighter? *Police Practice and Research*, *3*(4), 287–304. https://doi.org/10.1080/1561426022000032060

U.S. Code, Title 22, Chapter 38, Paragraph 2656f (d)(2).

Walsh, J. I. (2013). The effectiveness of drone strikes in counterinsurgency and counterterrorism campaigns. Army War College, Carlisle Barracks Pa. Strategic Studies Institute.

Walter, E. V. (1969). *Terror and resistance*. Oxford University Press.

Weber, M. (1965). *Politics as a vocation*. Fortress Press.

APA uses the word "References." Other styles use other titles.

Alphabetize by the first letter of the first important word of every citation.

Double space page with no extra spacing between entries.

A hanging indent is the opposite of a normal indent. Everything after the first line is indented one-half inch or five spaces.

Many professors read the References list first to evaluate depth of research and attention to detail.

PERMISSIONS ACKNOWLEDGMENTS

Figure 1.1: Savage, Doug. "The Argument." *Savage Chickens*. Reproduced with permission of Doug Savage.

Figure 6.2: Savage, Doug. "New Evidence." *Savage Chickens*. Reproduced with permission of Doug Savage.

Figure 6.5: Savage, Doug. "In Moderation." *Savage Chickens*. Reproduced with permission of Doug Savage.

Figure 6.7: "Canadians on Citizenship." Reproduced courtesy of Environics Institute, Institute for Canadian Citizenship, Maytree foundation, CBC News, and RBC Royal Bank.

Figure 6.8a: Sanchez, Hugo. "Drawing the Lines of War: Avengers Age of Ultron." Reproduced with permission of Hugo Sanchez and Miguel Gomez.

Figure 6.8b: Lemonly. "Avengers, Assemble!" Reproduced with permission of Lemonly. www.lemonly.com.

Figure 6.11: Wildish, Stephen. "Euler Dietgram." Reproduced with permission of Stephen Wildish.

Figure 6.14: SoJones. "The History of Hip Hop" from "#AMAs The Ultimate History of Hip Hop." *SoJones*. https://sojones.com/news/105761-amas-the-ultimate-history-of-hip-hop-sojones-infographic.

Figure 6.19: Donnelly, Frank. "Distribution of US Public Libraries" from "Average Distance to Public Libraries in the US." *At These Coordinates*. https://atcoordinates. info/2016/02/22/average-distance-to-public-libraries-in-the-us. Reproduced with permission of Frank Donnelly.

INDEX

Note: Page numbers in *italics denote figures.*

From the Publisher

A name never says it all, but the word "Broadview" expresses a good deal of the philosophy behind our company. We are open to a broad range of academic approaches and political viewpoints. We pay attention to the broad impact book publishing and book printing has in the wider world; for some years now we have used 100% recycled paper for most titles. Our publishing program is internationally oriented and broad-ranging. Our individual titles often appeal to a broad readership too; many are of interest as much to general readers as to academics and students.

Founded in 1985, Broadview remains a fully independent company owned by its shareholders—not an imprint or subsidiary of a larger multinational.

For the most accurate information on our books (including information on pricing, editions, and formats) please visit our website at www.broadviewpress.com. Our print books and ebooks are also available for sale on our site.

broadview press
www.broadviewpress.com

This book is made of paper from well-managed FSC® - certified
forests, recycled materials, and other controlled sources.

 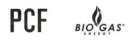